BLUEPRINT FOR LIFE

How To Survive and Thrive
in the Life Insurance Business

INDUSTRY newcomer or long-standing professional, independent intermediary or tied agent – all financial planners and managers will appreciate the immediate relevance of this book.

It is simultaneously a manual of sound business practice, a commonsense guide to customer psychology and the selling of life insurance and allied financial products, and a reference source of proven, workable sales ideas.

Provided you are prepared to accept the self discipline necessary for a successful career in this industry, then *Blueprint For Life* will always remain a valuable sales aid. Much like an old friend, it will continue to give inspiration, motivation, advice and sympathy.

By the same author

Employee Benefits in a
Modern Society

Selling Life My Way

Selling More Life My Way

Success Through Seminars

Blueprint For Life

How to Survive and Thrive
in the Life Insurance Business

Ken Clark FCII, FLIA

K.C. PROMOTIONS

First Published April 1991

ISBN : 0 9517400 0 8

Published by K.C. Promotions,
Hubbard House, Civic Drive
Ipswich, Suffolk IP1 2QA

Typeset, printed and bound in Great Britain
by J. Looker Printers Ltd, Dorset.
Editorial production by A & S Editors, Oxon.

ENTER THE WORLD
of the successful life insurance agent:

- a world of freedom, where an agent can be what he wants to be, do what he wants to do;
- a world of great financial rewards;
- a world of diversity, where no two days are alike;
- a world of excitement, travel, and honours;
- a world of honest friendships and the giving and sharing that go with them;
- a world of intensely-held beliefs;
- a world of tender joys and deeply felt sorrows;
- a world that challenges the mind and commits the heart.

Acknowledgements

UNWITTINGLY, MANY HUNDREDS of people from 44 countries across the world have contributed to this book. They are the members of the Million Dollar Round Table and the life insurance industry who have shared their best ideas with me, and I acknowledge and thank them for their contribution to my life.

No one achieves goals on their own. Over the years I have been singularly fortunate to have had quite outstanding people work for me whose loyalty, support and dedication I treasure.

I thank my editor and co-publisher Stewart Farr, who has by now read some 100,000 of my written words. He it was who encouraged me to write this book, and has proved a wonderful sounding board for my ideas.

Contents

PROLOGUE

"*OUR FINAL SPEAKER* this morning is Ken Clark. Ken started his career in the insurance industry in 1949 as the most junior clerk in the Accident Department of the Alliance Assurance Company in Queen Street, Ipswich."

Standing in the darkened wings of the theatre I listened to the familiar words which I had heard many times before. In some strange way it was as though the day chairman was talking about someone else, a stranger. Was this the same person who walked timidly into a Victorian building at the age of 17, on St. Valentine's Day 1949, and who was about to step out and address an audience of around 2,000 life assurance agents? At that moment Ipswich really did seem a very long way away from Surfers Paradise, Australia, where the scene was taking place.

One thing was certain. On that Monday morning four decades and more ago, this most junior of juniors could never have imagined he would one day find himself on the other side of the world about to make a major speech. Undoubtedly, all my superiors from those bygone days would have been equally surprised — indeed astonished would probably be a more appropriate word!

It was Australia's BiCentennial year, and I started my presentation by telling the story of a 39 year old servant girl from Ipswich, who close on 200 years before had been transported to Australia as one of the first Pohms, for what we would today consider comparatively trivial crimes. Over the next 18 years of her life she became known as one of the great chroniclers of early Australian life, and the many letters she wrote back to England were subsequently published in book form. I suspect her English friends and her employers (whose descendants still live in Ipswich) were as surprised at what she had achieved as were the people who knew me in my early days.

As I was telling the story of Margaret Catchpole, another part of my mind was wandering, asking questions. What brought about the change in Margaret Catchpole? How did it all come about? Were there any lessons which could be helpful to people today?

I have to confess I have not pursued this line of enquiry any further, much though I am fascinated by the life of this Ipswich girl. It is still to be found on my long list of goals to be achieved.

In the following months, everytime I listened to my introduction prior to a presentation, I found myself, more and more, thinking about my own situation, and my thoughts were crystallized when somebody said to me one day: "Ken, you have been fortunate enough to have so many experiences during your business career, and I am sure a lot of people could profit from some of the lessons you could pass on to them. The new man could hardly fail to benefit, and the 'old stagers' would be reminded of so many things they had forgotten."

My early ambition as a schoolboy was to be a journalist, but I was put off by the then editor of the *Daily Mail.* He told me I needed a University degree, and frankly, I knew I was not bright enough to pass the entrance exam! I finished up working for an insurance company simply because my father knew someone in the office and asked whether there was an opening for a young lad. There was, and I started to learn the mysteries of the insurance business with all thoughts of becoming a journalist being put on one side. Instead, I found out about no-claim discounts, legal liabilities, the law of accident insurance, insurance accounts and finance, and many other fascinating subjects.

I was very fortunate to have some excellent teachers in my office, of whom perhaps the Assistant Manager, Robin Cossons, was the best example. He it was who taught me letter writing. He had infinite patience and wisdom, and was without doubt my mentor.

Robin delighted in telling me how in his early days as an inspector of agents he was not provided with a company car but a horse, upon which he would set out to visit far flung parts of Suffolk where our loyal introducers were to be found. Totally dedicated to the business, Robin could be like an absent-minded professor, and many a time I and another junior were despatched around Ipswich to try and find his car because he could not remember where he had parked it!

After a few months I decided the inspectors with company cars had the best job of all because they were out and about most of the day, selling the company's products to agents and the public. Six years later, at the age of 24, I joined their club, becoming one of the company's youngest ever; I have continued on the sales side since.

Qualifying for the Million Dollar Round Table, setting up and being involved to this day with the Life Insurance Association, and running a direct sales branch has given me unique opportunities to meet with the top salespeople in our industry from all over the world. Indeed, I have been fortunate enough to appear on platforms with many of them, and whatever I have achieved has been very much due to the ideas and inspiration I have received from these role models. I have inherited their willingness to pass on to others what I have learned along the way. Like them I feel it part of my responsibility, because by so doing I can repay the great debt I have to the many hundreds of life assurance people who knowingly or unknowingly have helped me.

The wheel thus turns full circle. The business which has given me my career, now enables me to fulfil my original ambition of being a writer. I count myself extremely fortunate that the editor of the *Daily Mail* turned me down and dissuaded me from becoming a reporter. My career has, I am certain, been far more interesting, and dare I say useful, and has certainly taken me to places which never figured in the wildest daydreams I may have had as I wandered around Ipswich, delivering the previous day's letters to the business houses in the town all those years ago.

Writing for life assurance salespeople enables me to fulfil one of my lifelong ambitions. I hope that what I write will help you to achieve yours.

CHAPTER 1

Building a Financial Practice

MOST OF THE IMPORTANT lessons in life we learn through experience, often bitter and frequently too late. If only we would listen to what other people tell us. Even more important, if only we knew what were the right questions to ask!

When I started out as a life inspector I had a limited vision of my role. I saw my function as merely to produce as much life assurance, pensions and endowment business as I could for the branch, and to ensure I beat my annual target.

In 1965 I started my own composite brokerage. My very simple belief was to produce sufficient business to provide a satisfactory income for myself and any staff I employed. Having my own company was just a convenient way to operate. Many years were to pass before I realised I should have been focusing from the beginning on building a financial practice. I was not just a salesman, I was a businessman, and if only I had fully understood that from the beginning.

Sadly, even to this day the life insurance industry generally fails to include anything on this subject in its training programmes; it is one of the reasons for the continuing high and unacceptable failure rate. Despite all our sophisticated training programmes the failure rate today is almost exactly the same as it was 50 years ago, and clearly, something fundamental is missing. Part of the problem, of course, is to be found in the selection process, but far more is down to the early training and support packages offered by the industry.

Simply going out into the market place to factfind, give best advice and sell is not enough. Important though they are, unless you first think about what it means to be a businessman, you are putting the cart before the horse. Time and again I have looked at businesses which are failing, and recognised the same problem. People do not realise they are building not one but two companies when they are running their own business. The first is the one which manufactures the product or provides the service, and in this area the proprietors tend to be highly skilled. Frankly, it is rare you find a business that fails because the principals lack technical knowledge about their product.

The second business being created is what I would call a money company, and it is this which too many people fail to appreciate. It is the money company which gets into trouble through ignorance and naivety and ultimately drags the enterprise to the ground.

When I have been prospecting through the balance sheet, on more than one occasion I have had a company director say to me: "Ken, you know more about my company than I do." That always worries me because it is a classic example of a man not appreciating what is happening in his 'money company'.

Look around you and identify a successfully run private business. What are some of the characteristics you will find in the principals?

They will certainly have a marketing strategy. There is nothing haphazard about the way they set out to sell their products or services. They have clearly identified the market place within which they wish to operate, and it is the focus of their attention. To put it another way, they use the rifle shot approach rather than the shotgun. It has been my experience that the majority of salespersons start off with the shotgun, pointing it in the general direction of the public, pulling the trigger and hoping they hit something. It is only when they learn to target market that they really begin to become successful.

The successful businessman has clear objectives. He knows where he is going and how he is going to get there. He has a high drive and energy level, he is self confident, sets himself challenging but realistic goals, and is not afraid to risk the chance of failure.

The most important characteristic however, common to all, is that he has a business plan. It will start with a Mission Statement and continue by setting out in detail how it will be achieved. A fundamental part of it will comprise the cash flow budgets showing anticipated expenses on a month by month basis which clearly demonstrates what income is required. This determines the level of business or volumes of sales which must be produced in order to stay solvent, and provides the basis for their entire operation.

This just does not happen in our industry. The new entrant is encouraged to think solely in terms of new business production, but that is no measure of cash flow. I have known people qualify for the Million Dollar Round Table and yet not be able to afford the air fare to go to the Annual Meeting.

It is no good having a plan without a monitoring system. I designed my own and have used it for many years. It has the advantage of being simple, and therefore it takes little time to complete, yet provides all the information I need to monitor my practice against my pre-set plans. Having worked out what I need or want to produce in income terms in a 12 month period, I translate this into production, using the statistics I have built up over previous years. I know how many cases I need to produce in order to generate the income I require, and I keep a record of each one I write. This application register allows me to see at a glance the status of any particular application, and, of course, my objective is to get each one in-force in the shortest possible time. A piece of graph paper with my target line shows me where I should be, and a monthly update tells me where I am. When I fall below the line I know it is time to increase my activity.

If you are running your own business it is important to do your bookwork on a monthly basis, reconciling your bank statements and checking you have received all the commission to which you are entitled. Even computers make mistakes when they are fed the wrong information; they are rarely, if ever, in your favour!

Preparation of a business plan is not something you do in five minutes on the back of an envelope. To do it properly will take about two days, and whether you are a new agent just embarking on your career or have years of experience behind you, the need is the same. If you fail to plan you are without doubt planning to fail — and at that you will almost certainly be successful.

CHAPTER 2

Developing a Marketing Strategy

"I *SELL LIFE INSURANCE*". Is that what you tell people when they ask what you do for a living? If so, you are selling yourself short and understating the true situation because we do much more than that — or we should.

Our product is unusual because it is intangible. In the truest sense of the word people cannot use it, and more often than not the client is not around to see the real benefit of what he has bought. Buy a new motor car and four of your five basic senses will immediately feel some benefit and satisfaction. Buy a life insurance policy and you certainly cannot touch, smell, hear or taste it! However, if it has been properly marketed the client should 'see' the real benefit, and indeed that should be his motivation for buying.

This brings me to something quite fundamental to our business today, a concept which is a vital ingredient to enhance the likelihood of success in building our financial practice in the next decade.

In the past we have been seen, and probably seen ourselves as salespeople; indeed, there were some organisations who gave their sales forces only one or two products and expected them to sell nothing else.

Even before the Financial Services Act came into force in 1986, people were realising there had to be a change. The public was beginning to expect more comprehensive advice from financial advisers, and it was also obvious the people who really succeeded were those who painted on a much broader canvas. Selling products is no longer good enough. We have to focus on marketing our services. But first of all it is essential to understand the difference between selling and marketing.

As long ago as 1975 in the '*Harvard Business Review*', Theodore Levitt, a Harvard Business School professor, and a speaker at LIMRA schools, wrote an article in which he said: "Selling focuses on the needs of the seller, marketing on the needs of the buyer. Selling is preoccupied with the seller's need to convert his product into cash; marketing is concerned with the idea of satisfying the needs of the customer by means of the product, and a whole cluster of things associated with creating, delivering and finally consuming it. In short, the organisation must learn to think of itself not as producing goods or services, but as buying customers, as doing the things that will make people want to do business with it." More about that in Chapter 4 on Fact-finding, but it does lead on to the next crucial point which is Target Marketing, defined as the identification of a specific market or markets which you wish to penetrate. To do so you need to create and implement an action plan, always with the aim of satisfying the needs of the customer.

Research has shown that those agents who are consistently successful do have an identifiable market. Familiarity with the market breeds confidence which in turn enhances an agent's performance. Success in that market helps to establish a reputation which will precede the agent, and facilitate an approach to other members of the same market.

CHARACTERISTICS OF A TARGET MARKET

A good target market has five characteristics.

1. It must be large enough. Penetrating a market takes a lot of work, and an agent must learn everything he can about it. The last thing you want is for your market to run dry of prospects just when you have had a chance to get into it.

Niche marketing is all very well for the very experienced agent, and we will see more people focusing on highly selective quality markets in the future. However, until you have the qualifications to deal in these very specialised areas you need to focus your attention on large banks of prospects.

2. It should be geographically concentrated. Economics and time planning surely dictate the majority of your market should be within 40 miles of your place of work. If you are concentrating on a market where prospects are thinly spread from one end of the country to another you will not be able to achieve the required number of daily appointments — and will be wasting most of your time sitting behind the wheel of your car.

You are also less likely to build up a reputation within your selected market, and the availability of recommendations and introductions will be limited.

3. It has to be a market you can get into easily. For example, the new agent who decides to focus on the chief executive officers of the 200 top companies in his catchment area might find it difficult to break in and make appointments. He could be perceived as lacking credibility and reputation. On the other hand, as a self employed businessman himself he will be able to identify with shopkeepers, plumbers, carpenters and plasterers of whom there are many around.

4. The market must be permanent. 'Win Plans' based on one off opportunities, perhaps inspired by Government legislation, are all very well, but they do not form the basis of a successful business. They should be looked upon as a window of opportunity. For consistent business production, you must have a reliable, ever present, unlimited number of qualified prospects in your market place.

5. The market should be one in which the agent is comfortable. You need to feel an expert in it yourself because that will give you confidence. For example, let us say you decide to focus on farmers. You should be listening to the '*Farming Programme*' on Radio 4 every morning to become familiar with what's going on. It would be advisable to take out a subscription to an agricultural journal, and you might even want to advertise in it. When you feel sufficiently qualified, submit an article on some particular subject — perhaps inheritance tax planning.

Go to livestock sales throughout your area and be seen at markets on a regular basis. Learn the jargon and make your presentation using language the farmer can relate to.

Purely as an example, mortgages are an obvious target market. They have all the characteristics, and can certainly form the basis, of a successful practice. I know because it was the foundation for my business. Even in a slump houses are still changing hands, and probably eight out of ten purchasers need a mortgage.

New prospects are automatic. Unless he is a first time buyer, someone purchasing a property is also selling one. Thus there are at least three people involved in the chain, and possibly many more. I recall one time when I was involved in a chain of 22, all of whom came from just one introduction.

After placing over 200 mortgages in my best year, I decided the time had come to shift markets, and I began to develop the clients I already had. Many of those early mortgage clients are still with me, not only buying and selling houses, but running their own businesses, becoming wealthy, needing pension products, inheritance tax planning, and the whole range of services which our industry can offer them.

IDENTIFYING YOUR MARKET

Veterans in the business are fortunate. They have an existing client bank which may already be focused primarily in one particular business market. To you, I would say start by analysing your existing client base to see if there is a pattern. There are some questions to which you need answers:

1. Who are your existing clients?
2. What are their economic circumstances?
3. How did you find them?
4. Has serving them been profitable to you?
5. Are you comfortable working with them?
6. Do they respond to your suggestions in a positive way?
7. Are they convenient to you geographically to make it worth your while to continue to serve them — or could they provide you with recommendations and introductions?

As a result of this analysis you will be able to divide your clients into three categories. Category 'A' are those from whom you get positive answers to all your questions. They are clearly key clients, your real assets. Category 'B' are those who fail on one or more of your questions, but who you believe could satisfy your Category 'A' definition in the future; whilst Category 'C' fail on the majority of your questions, and should be regarded as mere policyholders.

In Chapter 7 I have described in some detail what I have done in order to provide a high level of service to my existing clients and shown how I isolate and focus on one of my target markets.

THE NEW AGENT

What does the new agent do? He has no client bank to work on, and therefore, at first sight target marketing looks impossible. Not so. He may not have a client bank, but he certainly has a network and this becomes his target market.

The members of his network are all those people who know him. Relatives, friends, business associates, customers, tradesmen, even old school friends. With everyone in his network he has a particular advantage. They know him and there is no doubt at all people buy from people. What he lacks in experience he can make up for by using his personal contacts to provide a stream of receptive prospects.

OUR MARKETING EDGE

Whilst we suffer from what some people say to be the disadvantage of selling intangibles, we have the advantage of a wide product range. If you are selling computers you are only marketing one product. When you are in financial services you are marketing a range of solutions to many financial problems and no one product will solve them all.

You cannot build a successful financial practice nowadays on hit and miss methods. A carefully thought out marketing strategy is as vital for us as it always has been for most other industries. We are just a few years late in getting into it, and whilst we have been able to survive with the 'back of an envelope' approach in the past, it will not do for the future.

CHAPTER 3

If You Have No Prospects – You Have No Prospects

PILOTING A LIGHT AIRCRAFT one day, I took off from Kidlington aiming for my airfield in Suffolk. It was a Saturday afternoon in September and visibility was reduced by the clouds of smoke from burning stubble fields. Engrossed in conversation with my passenger, after an hour I realised we were lost. Normally, that would not be a problem because there is usually a friendly RAF station with its radar scanners to help you out. Not on a Saturday afternoon however. That was not the worst problem though. I had made a potentially fatal mistake and failed to fill up with petrol before we left Oxfordshire.

Low in fuel we eventually landed in a recently harvested field, found out from the nearest village where we were, worked out a new heading, and some 20 minutes later very thankfully put the aeroplane down on the familiar runway.

I was lucky; I walked away from what could have been disaster, and my career as pilot — and indeed as a life insurance salesperson — could have come to an end.

The moral of the story is, you must always keep your tank full. That applies whether you are flying an aeroplane, driving your car or building a financial practice.

In the latter case the fuel is represented by your bank of prospects. Allow it to run dry and your career will come to a very abrupt and quite painful end!

I do not believe anyone is born a natural prospector. You have to develop habits so that it becomes routine, and you then do it without even thinking about it. To get to that stage certainly requires a lot of discipline, but attitude of mind is even more important.

Many of the sales training books I have read recommend setting aside an hour a day for prospecting. I have to disagree. You should be prospecting every minute of every day, and the reason is quite simple.

The people who need our products and services are all around us 24 hours a day, not just for the one hour we decide to look for them.

One of the industry greats, John Savage, says, "No one has a prospecting problem because the world is full of them. What they have is an approach problem." Ron Barbaro, now Chief Executive of the mighty Prudential of America says the same thing in a slightly different way: "Prospecting is all about meeting people under favourable circumstances."

WHO IS THE IDEAL PROSPECT?

A prospect has been defined as someone who has a need, the ability to pay and to pass the medical and with whom it is possible for us to get an appointment. I disagree with that statement too. The ideal prospect is not the person I want to see, but the person who wants to see me. I want to spend my business life talking to people who are really interested in what I have to say, and preferably have invited me to talk to them.

That philosophy immediately rules out all the forms of cold calling, be it door knocking, telephone sessions or clipboard style interviews. I find those methods distasteful, unprofessional, frustrating, depressing, uneconomic and undignified. It is no wonder our industry at times is pilloried in the press. Adopting cold calling methods of prospecting is simply shooting yourself in the foot, and in any event, is totally unnecessary.

The fact is, we market fabulous products and services which the public desperately need. The problem is, they do not usually realise it until they give the opportunity to a well trained life insurance agent to sit down and talk with them about their needs. Sometimes I feel we have products that everybody needs but nobody wants. Our job is to make them want what they need, but first you have to get in front of them. How is it done?

Let us start with what is known as the domestic market. Assuming you believe in the value of our product and services, and the contribution they can make to the quality of life of people around you, to whom should you first talk? Surely, your relatives and friends? We have the greatest possible responsibility to protect them against the worst that life can sometimes bring. Can you imagine how devastated you would feel if your brother lost the ability to earn his living through a catastrophic accident, and you had not talked to him about permanent health insurance? The feeling of guilt would stay with you for the rest of your life.

Sadly, the majority of agents tell me they have not approached their relatives or friends because they "don't want to get a reputation of always trying to sell insurance." I have to question whether people like that should really be in our business.

Now it may well be your brother is married and his wife, of course, has a family as well — a mother, father and other brothers and sisters. You should know their circumstances and be aware of their special needs. Do you anticipate any difficulty in getting an introduction? I do not think you will have a problem if you will only ask — the classic 'referral'.

THE FAMILY NETWORK

Take this a step or two further. Every prospect you talk to has a family network. As part of your factfind you should find out about it. Most companies' factfind forms have a section headed 'Families and Relatives', or something similar. The majority of agents consider that simply means partner's name and age, and details of their children. Not so; it means all their relatives, and could generate a minimum of six introductions to people whom you can meet under the most favourable circumstances possible.

However, not only does your prospect have a family network, he may well have a circle of business acquaintances as well. A properly conducted factfind interview could shake out several more people for you to see.

I know most agents feel embarrassed about asking for referrals. I understand that because I have the same feeling myself. Paradoxically, most of my new clients are actually referred to me in one way or another, but thankfully they come automatically because of the way in which I work.

Let us look at one or two other examples of very effective prospecting techniques.

"John, tell me, if you were applying for a job today and were required to provide two references, who would they be?" John will now tell you the names of the two people who he knows hold him in the highest possible regard. "Tell me something about them, John", and he will without even asking why you want to know. You are doing some preliminary factfinding. Let us assume he says, "Well, Bill is married to Mary and they have two children, he runs his own small company writing computer programmes. They recently bought a house on the Springfield Estate." Surely there is enough there for you to say to John: "You know, he sounds the sort of person who might well benefit from a conversation with me, will you give me an introduction?"

Simple, effective and very easy to do. Two additional names and introductions from every meeting.

What about the assistant manager in the hotel where you have lunch from time to time. "Would you mind if I asked you three questions? Would I be right in assuming you have a mortgage?"

Eight times out of 10 you would be right.

"Would I also be right in assuming you have covered the loan with life assurance so that it would be paid off in the event of your death?"

Again eight out of 10 times you'll be right.

"Last question. Would I likewise be right in assuming that if you lost the ability to earn your living through accident or illness you would have extreme difficulty in maintaining your mortgage payments, and you have done nothing about it?" You know the statistics by now, don't you? Eight out of 10 times you will be right.

"Let's sit down tomorrow when you come off duty, and I'll show you what you need to do."

MOVING UP-MARKET

So you are in the corporate market or maybe want to get into it. Is there any difference?

Not really, because after all every big businessman is almost certainly a husband and a father, so he has all the domestic insurance needs of everybody else. However, he is almost certain to have a business network you can tap into. Perhaps it is the suppliers he uses, or the customers to whom he sells. It may be other firms with whom he finds himself working on a contract. For example, an electrician is certain to know plumbers, bricklayers, glaziers, architects, roofing specialists, landscape gardeners and a lot of other electricians. A plumber would have a similar circle of contacts and so on. Properly approached, they can give you the qualified introduction you need which will virtually guarantee you an appointment.

"Birds of a feather flock together". To put it another way, find out where businessmen congregate and join the congregation!

Some years ago I purchased a ticket and attended as a delegate a seminar on venture capital put on by a very large firm of accountants. I reasoned that the majority of people in the audience were looking for venture capital, otherwise why would they be there? Those were the sort of people I wanted to meet because clearly they were expansion-minded entrepreneurs.

How right I was. I met my first prospect standing in the queue for coffee and within 10 days I had set up for him a self administered pension scheme for a very substantial initial contribution.

As at all good conferences, everyone who attended was given a list of delegates, and they were so easy to approach. No way was that cold prospecting. I knew them, they knew me, I knew what they were interested in and they thought I might be able to help them. The ideal prospects — people who wanted to see me!

Of course, one of the best ways to ensure you spend time with a nest of businessmen, wherever they happen to meet, is to organise the meeting yourself; this brings me to my very successful Breakfast Club.

We have been meeting on the first Wednesday of every month since 1976. Around two dozen of us foregather at 7 am and breakfast is served at 7.30. At 8 am any guests are introduced by their host and given a brief moment to talk about themselves. We then have a guest speaker who has until 9 am, during which time he or she can talk, ask questions, lead a discussion or do whatever he/she feels like.

Our speakers have ranged over the most varied subjects possible — from a woman scientist who told us of the difficulties of getting fresh water to Saudi Arabia by towing an iceberg from the Antarctic, to Lord Belstead describing the role of the Leader of the House of Lords. We even had a lady demonstrating medieval embroidery, who gave one of the most fascinating talks we have ever had.

This breakfast club is a network of the highest quality. I started it by inviting a dozen or so businessmen to "Stretch their day" by meeting once a month with like-minded business people over breakfast. The idea was to exchange ideas that might be mutually beneficial in developing our respective businesses. Since then we have expanded our membership, but retained one of our original 'rules' that we will only have one person from any particular trade, industry or profession. This ensures we have no conflicts or clashes.

We can even use the breakfast club to meet particular people we might otherwise have found difficulty in approaching. All we have to do is ring them up and invite them to speak. Our reputation is such that they never turn us down. They want to speak to us, little realising that we also may want to speak to them!

The business which passes between the members is quite amazing. One of our rules is that we must never try to sell to fellow members. If they want anything they have to ask. Back to my ideal prospect or client — someone who wants to talk to me.

BUSINESS DINNERS

If you are not an early morning person, what about dinners? Select three corporate clients and invite them to dinner. Give them the opportunity of bringing a guest.

On the night you are simply the host. "Gentlemen, there are four reasons why we are meeting together tonight. First of all, I wanted to spend time with three of my clients away from their place of work. Second, I wanted to meet three of their friends. Third, I wanted you to meet each other because quite often relationships will be formed which can be beneficial to all in the future. Finally, we are going to have a really enjoyable dinner together."

That is all I say about business. My three clients will do all the work for me. They will tell their guests who I am, what I can do for them, and because they are my guests everything they say will be complimentary. How easy it is in a month or so to call the guests and ask for an opportunity to have a business meeting. It is not surprising they never say no!

The more sporting minded of my friends will arrange a golf day on a similar basis, or perhaps take a box at Lords, Wimbledon or at the local football ground. It doesn't matter what it is as long as you can bring together a group of like-minded business people who subsequently will want to meet you again!

SEMINAR PROSPECTING IS THE MARKETING CONCEPT FOR THE FUTURE

How would you like to stand before a group of people who you know are really keen to hear what you have to say on a variety of financial topics? That is what happens when you put on a seminar, and I can tell you, it's a great feeling!

Prospecting through seminars is the marketing concept for the future. The day of the '100 letters a week' mail shot are over — the public really are rebelling against junk mail. Equally, they do not react favourably to the telephone approach at home in the evening when they have just settled down to watch their favourite television programme. Think about it — how do you feel about it if someone does it to you?

The delightful thing about seminars is that everyone who accepts your invitation clearly meets the basic criteria of the ideal prospect; they want to see you, and you meet 'under favourable circumstances'. Provided you put on a quality seminar, your success rate in turning the attendees into clients will be very high.

Seminar prospecting deserves a book of its own because you have to get everything right. If you need to know more there is an excellent publication entitled '*Success Through Seminars*' written by Kenneth Clark!!!*

A CONSTANT NEED

Prospecting is not just for the new people in the industry. The experienced agent may not appear to be continually prospecting, but don't be fooled. He or she has just made it a totally routine habit, as automatic as getting up in the morning and going to bed at night. It will be very rare to meet someone who has bought the last life insurance, pensions, investment, saving plan or annuity that he is ever going to purchase. As a result he/she is a prospect — if not for today, for tomorrow.

One of Clark's Laws is that a prospect is a client who has not yet bought from you. When you view everybody you meet in the light of that statement, your attitude to this most important part of our job can only change for the better.

Remember, the most highly trained life insurance salesperson with no prospects is like Concorde with no fuel — neither has the energy to get off the ground.

* Available direct from the author — £16 inc: P&P

CHAPTER 4

Factfinding

IT MAKES A LOT of sense to go to the dentist every six months for a regular check-up. How many times have you sat in the dentist's chair confident nothing was wrong until his gentle probe sent an exquisite pain through the top of your head — to reveal you had a problem? You instantly suffer mixed emotions! Sadness that there is a problem, apprehension about what it is going to cost you in pain, and yet a feeling almost of resignation that the job has to be done. When you walk out 20 minutes later and the work has been done you feel on cloud nine, of course!

That could actually be the description of a really good factfind. The majority of our prospects and clients believe that before we start talking about their insurance and pensions programme it is adequate. Our objective is to help them discover otherwise if that is not the case. Our conversation should take them along a voyage of discovery, during which we gently point out to them items of interest where, hopefully, they will want to stop and investigate further.

Many new agents find this process somewhat daunting. They come off training courses, armed with a pile of eight-page factfind forms, some of which they have filled in during role play sessions. They are aware the Financial Services Act requires them to 'know their client', which is interpreted to mean 'ask a lot of questions'. Well, we certainly do have to know our clients, but what is even more important is for our clients to get to know themselves. Only then will they buy; only then will they remain committed on a long term basis to the solutions they have purchased for the problems they have uncovered during a meeting with us.

I regard a first interview with a prospective client — or a review meeting with an existing client — as a 'getting to know you' occasion. With the new prospect the beginnings of a relationship have to be established. My good friend, Charles McCann puts it this way: "At a first meeting the prospective client has three questions in his mind which he probably never asks, but to which he certainly requires the answers."

Question 1. "Can I trust this person."
Question 2. "Does he or she know the subject."
Question 3 "Are they putting themselves first, or me first."

The only way you can answer those questions satisfactorily is to know the answers yourself. Your sole objective in being in front of your new prospect is to help him become aware of the problems he has, then to design the solutions for those he considers important enough to require action.

As you are getting to know him, he is getting to know you. Only if he trusts you will he open the window on his financial life and allow you to look through. All we are really marketing is trust. If they don't trust you they will not buy from you.

Even with an existing client on an annual review, the 'getting to know you' process is vital. Time has gone by since your last meeting; your client has changed, you have changed. You have to re-establish your relationship before you can expect true communication — which is a two way process — to begin. Until it does you will just be talking to each other.

When I was attempting to build a relationship with professional advisers in my locality, I actually invited them to what I called 'Getting to know you lunches'. My approach was simple. "It would be nice to if we could build a relationship which could be mutually beneficial, but I appreciate we know very little about each other. I would like to invite you to a 'Getting to know you lunch' which would enable us to establish whether there is a basis of an understanding which would enable us to work together in the future."

One particular firm of solicitors grilled me for 45 minutes over lunch. I was delighted; that was exactly what I wanted, and I obviously passed the test for sometime later they asked if I would be prepared to give advice on their partnership agreement because everytime they met to discuss it they ended up fighting!

HARD FACTS — SOFT FACTS

Whenever two people have a conversation they exchange both hard and soft facts. "Hello John, where are you living now?" — hard fact. "What do you like about the area where you live?" — soft fact.

Hard facts are factual; soft facts are feelings and opinions. Soft facts tell you and the prospect what the problem is, whilst hard facts determine the size of it.

The soft facts are by far and away the most important. Strangely enough, your prospective client will almost certainly know most, if not all, of the hard facts about himself, but may not be so clear on the soft facts. Perhaps he has never really thought about them before. For example, you could say to him, "What is your attitude to life assurance?" The chances are no one has ever asked him that question before and so he has not really thought about it. He may well respond, "I don't understand what you mean." "Well tell me, do you have any?" If he says yes, you can follow up by saying, "Why did you buy it?" He will probably say something about protecting his family. "What do you mean by protecting them?" "Well to provide some cash for them in the event of my death."

Now you are into a really good factfind interview, because whilst you are asking the questions, your prospect's mind is racing ahead of you. He is likely to realise that however much life assurance he has got, it will be inadequate to do what he wants it to do; and you have not even got to that stage yet.

This technique is part of what is known as the Broad Concept Interview which, I believe, goes way back to Socrates. He it was who developed what became known as the Socratic Interview — a method of 'systematic doubt and questioning'.

"John, let me ask a question. If you had died yesterday what income would Mary have today?" Question 1 of the Broad Concept. Now your prospect (or client) may well not be sure of the hard fact answer, but he certainly knows the soft fact — it won't be enough, and you haven't even asked the second question: "What income would you like her to have?"

In simple terms, for a man who cares for his family the answer will be exactly the same income as he has now — and he's already anticipating your third question. "John, how will Mary make up the difference?" This is the tough one, and your prospective client moves into a compromise mode. "Well, she would probably have to sell the house." "Yes John, that's an alternative, is that what you would want her to do?" It probably isn't, and so you ask him what other alternatives he can suggest. Go back to work, take in lodgers, move back to her parents — and perhaps as a last resort he might even say to you: "I suppose you are going to tell me the answer would be to buy some more life assurance?" Whatever he says, your response is the same.

"Yes John, that is an alternative, is that what you would want to happen?" If you conduct the interview properly he will actually bring up the question of life assurance before you do!

Question four is simple. "John, of all the alternatives, which is the one you find most acceptable today?" Quite frequently, purchasing further life assurance proves to be his choice, and then it's a question of getting down to the hard facts, and determining how much.

Exactly the same format can be used when you get around to the pensions position or income protection, and it is equally applicable to the business market. For example, you're with two partners running an estate agency, "John, if your partner Fred had died last night what would be happening to his share in your partnership today?" The chances are he will not be too sure of the answer, but eventually he may decide it would be passed on to Fred's widow.

Question 2. "What would you want to be happening to Fred's share?" Almost certainly John would want to buy it. "How would you raise the money?" Borrow from the bank, raise a mortgage on the house, sell some assets or perhaps purchase the share by instalments of capital. "If there was another alternative that would cost you now between 1 per cent and 2 per cent a year would you find that attractive?"

Properly used, the Broad Concept is the basis of a classic 'getting to know you' interview, enabling you to give undoubted 'best advice'. This I interpret to mean producing the right solutions for what the client thinks are his biggest problems.

HOW TO GET STARTED

The classic way to start an interview with a brand new client is for you first to tell him something about yourself. Who you are, the company you represent, whether you are a tied agent or an independent intermediary, how long you have been in the business and so on. Then it is perfectly natural to say, "Now tell me something about yourself." All you have to do then is sit back and make maximum use of your eyes and ears and minimum use of your mouth! You want to listen and watch more than you talk. I am not an advocate of the use of scripts but nevertheless you need to have in your mind a very clear framework for your interview. Just become familiar with the main headings on your factfind form, like personal details of family, employment, property ownership and mortgages, life assurance programme, pensions provision, investments and savings, personal assets, business assets, inheritance tax and financial objectives.

Armed with that framework, a good memory and an A4 pad, you can conduct a first class interview with anybody.

There is an alternative way which I find very successful, and that is to take the financial objectives section of the normal factfind form and, 'blow it up' on the photocopier. Give it to your prospect at the beginning of your interview and ask him to spend a few moments considering what are his objectives, and their priority order. When he gives the form back to you, do not look at it. Get into your conversation and when you feel you and he have both found out as much as you can, turn to the objectives form and say: "John, at the beginning of our conversation you prioritised your financial objectives and number one was financial security for your family. In the light of the conversation we have just had, do you think you are achieving whatever you mean by that statement?" If he says no, you use the hard facts to help you design your solution.

A further alternative I have heard advocated is to focus on the hard facts right at the beginning. "John, I need to get some basic information before I can begin to talk about your situation, so if you don't mind I would just like to ask you a number of personal questions." You then proceed to fill in the statistical part of your factfind as though it were a mortgage application, drawing no conclusions whatsoever from the information provided. When you have completed it, you put it on one side and follow by saying, "Now you have given me the basic information let's go back to the beginning. Tell me something more about your children, your job, your opinion of education, your attitude to life assurance, your dreams, goals and ambitions."

Whichever method you use, at the conclusion you must be able to complete the factfind form, of course, because it will need to accompany any applications you might write. You will also know a great deal about your client, and he will about you. It is a very good discipline to make some comprehensive file notes which put flesh upon the skeleton framework of the hard facts. My practice is to 'talk' to my portable dictating machine as soon as I leave the prospect whilst the conversation is still fresh in my mind. This has a number of benefits.

First of all, I am summarising the key features of the meeting and recording the discussions we had and the decisions taken.

Second, when my secretary transcribes my dictation she becomes familiar with the client's case, and is better able to handle any problems which may arise whilst I am out of the office.

Third, 'if the inspector calls' from the regulatory body I can show that I have indeed got to know my client, and can establish the basis upon which I gave him what I considered to be my best advice. Finally, if the client has any doubt in the future as to the rationale behind the decisions taken, my file note will help resolve them.

KEY QUESTIONS

There are a number of key questions I like to include in all my meetings with prospects and clients. More than anything else they help me to understand the client, and more important, the client to understand himself.

"Tell me, what are the three things you value most in life?" Whether I ask that question to individuals or to audiences in any part of the world, I get the same answer every time: "Health, wealth and my family".

Somewhere during the interview I will ask, "If these areas are so important to you, what are you doing about them?" You will instantly realise our business focuses on all three. If a client's health fails we can step in with an income, we are in the wealth creating business, and we certainly protect families and businesses from the catastrophes of life.

The second key question is, "Tell me what are your three most important goals?" Now he may well give you the same answers, and that is even better, but the chances are he will have some objectives in life that he wants to achieve, and again, that is where we come in. We are in the business of helping people achieve their goals, dreams and ambitions.

The third key question is, "Tell me three things you have always wanted to do and haven't yet done?" His answers will give you a unique insight into the type of person you are dealing with.

THE RIPPLE EFFECT

If the phrase 'Socratic Interview' is more than you can tolerate, then what about the ripple effect?

Picture yourself standing on the shore of a lake. It is a beautiful calm day, and nothing is disturbing the surface of the water. Pick up a pebble and gently toss it away from you. As it hits the water there will be a splash lasting only a few seconds. From the splash will emanate a series of ripples, one behind the other, which will continue for perhaps two or three minutes until they reach the shore — making the reeds wave, and the ducks to gently ride up and down. If the ripples are strong enough they will actually damage the bank.

That is the way I see the conversations I have with my prospects and clients. The questions I ask them are like the splash of the pebble, but they are designed to set up a series of ripples, and it is those which will disturb, and hopefully, lead to action. I actually do not want to sell anything to my clients at all. I want them to buy from me. Remember, everybody needs our products but very few want to buy them. If the ripples do their job your prospect will become aware of the need, and develop the urge to buy.

At the end of your meeting he should feel he knows himself better than he did at the beginning. Talking to you should have been an enjoyable learning experience even if, like the visit to the dentist, some of the solutions have been both painful and somewhat costly.

Be aware, however, that people never tell you everything. Just like a personal computer there are always some hidden menus which they don't want to reveal to you. For many years I advised a businessman in Ipswich on all aspects of his financial planning in relation to his life assurance, pensions and investments — or so I thought. When he finally retired he asked me to meet with him to plan his retirement income, and then admitted he had very substantial shareholdings which went back many years, and which he had never told me about. He just felt it was information I did not need, or perhaps, he did not want me to have at the time.

We can only give people best advice based upon the information they are willing to give us. Our factfind needs to be as thorough as we can make it and, frankly, the better we are the more impressed the client. Think about your own situation. If you go to your doctor complaining of a pain and all he does is write out a prescription you would not be very impressed. If, on the other hand, he goes to enormous trouble in questioning you about the symptoms, the longer he goes on the more impressed you would be by him — and the more confidence you would have in his diagnosis and advice.

If we want to be regarded as professionals in our business we have to start performing like professionals. We will become more effective, and produce quality business with a high persistency level, and wonder of wonders, begin to get recommendations and introductions without even asking for them.

CHAPTER 5

Designing and Presenting Solutions

THERE ARE MANY different opinions on the number of steps in the sales process. LIMRA — the Life Insurance and Marketing Research Association — claims 10 and has published an excellent book which the new man in particular would find worth reading. *

Without doubt, however, the key steps must be factfinding and designing and presenting solutions. In the early days of direct sales forces the accent was very much upon making a sale at the first meeting. Agents were told "close seven times, don't take no for an answer, and make sure you walk out with a completed application for something." Managers were encouraged to believe they had recruited another failure if a new agent did not succeed in making sales on his first appointments.

Do not misunderstand me. There is nothing fundamentally wrong in making a sale at the first meeting, if the need is obvious and a client is ready to go ahead.

Here is the important point. It is a two stage process, and both could occur at the same interview. My belief is if the opportunity presents itself to close a sale you do so. If the client says to you, "It's all very well for you to talk to me about life assurance but what I really want to do at this time is start up a pension plan", then in my judgement the best advice you could give him is: "You get out your cheque book and I'll fill in the application and factfind."

* *'Steps Into Sales'* — published by LIMRA, Hartford, Connecticut, USA.

SIMPLE CASES REQUIRE SIMPLE SOLUTIONS

Cases fall into two categories — simple and complex. Strangely enough, both require the same solutions — simple ones — but the complex require a great deal more work before you are ready to come up with your recommendations.

I am a strong advocate that all recommendations should be put in writing. Even if you make a sale at a first meeting take my advice and write to the client afterwards. Tell him what he did, and why he did it, and incorporate any additional recommendations which you believe he should consider. More and more we must put things in writing. It is the way professionals work, and without doubt will help to cement your relationship and improve your persistency ratio.

Always be aware today's simple case may well develop into tomorrow's jumbo, and if that happens you want to make sure you remain the servicing agent. It is vital, therefore, to offer the same standard of excellence to all clients, although you clearly tailor make your presentation according to the nature of the case. A simple case may be over and done with in a month. Approach, first interview, factfind, brief report, completed business, policy delivered and the file away to store. Complex cases can take three months.

Agents, it is said, pass through three clearly identifiable stages as they develop their financial practice. The first is starry eyed optimism. We can all remember that one, although it was of short duration. Hopefully, we were left with the optimism after the stars faded!.

Stage two is sophisticated complication, and frankly, some agents never seem to leave it! You can always tell someone is at this level. They churn out endless pages of reports, closely typed, liberally peppered with a multitude of abbreviations like CGT, IHT, MIRAS to name but a few, leaving the reader totally bemused. Whilst he may possibly be impressed by the erudition of the author, he ultimately either takes no action at all or buys from someone else in language he understands.

Classic responses by prospects to these reports are, "This is really interesting. I must discuss it with my accountant" or, "Leave it with me I need to study it in detail". Don't believe either. What he is really saying is, "I don't understand all of this stuff, but I am not going to say so because you might think me an idiot". The longest such report I ever saw was 56 pages and included a bewildering array of projected year by year values of all the policies which the agent was recommending. Frankly, he lost me halfway down page 2, and I doubt whether his prospect got even that far!

Ideally it is advisable to make an appointment for a second meeting with your prospect before you leave the first, but if the case is complicated this may not be possible. Instead, explain the work you are going to undertake for your prospective client, and try to give him some idea of a timescale. For example, you almost certainly need to get valuations of all the existing policies with other insurance companies, and you will require his letter of authority. Gathering this information will take time but is an essential part of the process. You cannot possibly give best advice without taking into account pre-existing policies.

It makes sense to write to your prospect after your first meeting, thanking him for giving you the opportunity to examine his situation and confirming in simple terms what you now plan to do.

Priority should be given initially to collecting and analysing the product particulars of existing contracts. Never believe what prospects tell you, not because they deliberately lie, but because they do not know precisely what they have. For example, you may be told, "I have this policy with Acme Insurance providing me with cover of £100,000". When you look into it you find out it is a 20 year family income plan, providing £5,000 a year, and taken out 10 years ago. The cover today is only £50,000.

Your analysis will be factual and statistical. An example of a summary form you could use is shown opposite, and when it is completed send it to your prospective client without making any comments on how good or bad his programme is, and without drawing any conclusions. In most cases the message is obvious. There just isn't enough of anything. At this stage you could also send him a copy of your factfind inviting comment. Some of the ripples you set up during your first meeting may have reminded him of things he should have told you and now is the time to find out.

The use of computer programmes which extract information from the factfind, re-produce it and then prepare a summary together with a detailed analysis are in common use, and will become even more popular in the future. Excellent though these systems may be, they are only part of the process and do not take the place of individually produced reports.

My practice nowadays is to send the client a copy, explain it is the first printout, and ask him to make any changes necessary before I produce the final version. I know some agents take along the first version with their presentation at the second interview, but the

SUMMARY FORM

COMPANY	*POLICY NO*	*TYPE*	*PREMIUM*	*PAYABLE*	*SUM ASSURED*	*PROJECTED MATURITY BENEFITS DATE*	*NOTES*	*REASON FOR POLICY*

problem is, if there are any errors or omissions, the solutions will be inappropriate. Back to the drawing board, and it means a third meeting which is not good use of either your time, or your prospect's.

THE REPORT ITSELF

Complicated though the case might seem to be, your prospect's needs are quite simple. He has four questions he wants you to answer: What are my problems? How can I solve them? What's it going to cost? What's in it for me? I have now given you the framework for the entire presentation because you have to address yourself to those key issues in your report.

If you want to get your message over in a way that it can be understood, just remember those four questions and the four C's. You have to be clear, concise, complete and correct.

Clear, because the reader, your prospect, needs to be able to understand it at first reading. He may hold a First Class Honours degree in Electronic Engineering, but it doesn't mean he knows anything at all about life insurance, pensions and investment.

Concise, because it is a report in which the content is kept down to an intelligent and intelligible minimum. It is as long as it needs to be, and no longer. The art of precis which you learned at school should be practised!

Complete, because it must contain all the necessary information with nothing truly relevant left out, and even more important, nothing irrelevant left in.

Correct, because it is based on a very thorough factfind with every comment and conclusion qualified by the research you have undertaken.

Appearance and layout are extremely important and here you are, to some extent, in the hands of your secretary, if you are fortunate enough to have one. Make sure she or he understands precisely what you are trying to achieve, because an effective and attractive layout makes the report far easier to read, and is certainly more likely to be acted upon. Double line spacing is advisable with capital letters employed for key phrases. I must say the introduction of the word processor has been wonderful because you can see on the screen just what the final result will look like. In addition, you need to edit your report ruthlessly which may require several typings. In the days of the old fashioned typewriter I always felt guilty about having letters and reports re-typed because of the work involved, but now it is a piece of cake! There is no excuse for sloppy work with badly corrected mistakes. You can produce perfect results every time.

I start off my reports with an introduction which mainly comprises the financial objectives highlighted by my prospect in the initial interview. I state them very simply and without qualification. They are on a page by themselves and normally consist of a number of 'one liners'.

The second page is a summary of the recommendations I am proposing to make. Totally factual, no debate and no mention of cost. Traditionally, summaries have always appeared at the end of reports but I learned to do it the other way in my years as a Borough Councillor. Having a summary of the key recommendations first gave me an insight into a report which might run to 120 pages, and all I had to do in advance of any meetings was to scan them. I could rely on the officers to take me through it in detail at the meeting itself.

This is what I plan to happen with my prospective client.

The third page of my report is headed 'Rationale'. Here I deal with each individual objective individually, making some brief comment about what the prospect is planning to achieve, and explaining how my recommendation meets the objective. I use a separate page to deal with each specific area — protection, pensions, investments and so on. This way each page does not look too overwhelming and gives me the basis for my verbal presentation.

The next page is again purely factual, and comprises details of the premiums for each of my recommendations.

Then to the final page, which is headed 'Immediate Action'. There may well be more typing on this page than any other. I explain what applications we need to complete and why, and cover underwriting requirements, including examinations and ECG's. I will have a paragraph or two on the use of trusts, some advice on trustees and their responsibilities. Comments about fund choice, method of premium payment and so on will be included, and any other immediate action points necessary.

I always incorporate a paragraph headed 'Future Action'. Here I will talk about the needs to be acted upon at some stage in the future.

I believe in the use of appendices which really provide detailed background that might otherwise interrupt the flow of the report and cause confusion to the reader. It is much better to take out this detail work and put it at the back, referring to it as appropriate. For example, all policy illustrations are placed here, and will be referred to on page

4 dealing with contracts and costs. I also put samples of trust wordings and details of funds and fund performance in the appendix rather than clutter up the body of the report itself.

When completed the report is bound into a folder. I use the comb method with an attractive card cover; it really makes the whole thing look extremely professional.

MAKING THE PRESENTATION

If possible I try to have second meetings in my office because all the equipment is available. Should revised illustrations be required I can produce them at once. I just do not like carting my so-called portable computer around with me and I certainly try to avoid the need for a third interview before closing the business. The client has a copy of the report and so do I. I take him through it page by page and item by item, getting agreement as I go along. The report has been prepared in a logical sequence and there is no point in moving along if there is disagreement on anything you have said.

This is where the layout I have described is so helpful. Dealing as we can with each key area separately, makes it easier for the prospect to comprehend and inevitably produces multiple sales. Part of this is because the cost is kept away from the solution. Your prospective client must be able to judge the suitability of your solutions to his problems without being prejudiced by the costs involved. The time for compromise may come when you get to page 4, but then that really is his problem.

Our responsibility as advisers is to tell our client precisely and exactly what we believe he needs. His responsibility is to decide whether or not to do what we recommend. Our presentation should put him in the position of having all the information he needs upon which to base his final decision.

It has been my experience, almost without exception, that every time I produce a report of this type my prospective client proceeds with some, if not all, of my recommendations. My closing rate is virtually one to one. What is more, multiple sales are commonplace using this method.

However, this is not quite the end. The prospect may or may not take up all of my recommendations and the report I have prepared for him will, therefore, be inaccurate. In those circumstances I prepare a supplementary report in which I detail the action taken and why this is different from that originally recommended. Again the client has a copy and so do I.

His file is now complete; so is mine. I have a detailed factfind backed up by my own comprehensive notes arising out of the soft fact questions. There is an initial report containing best advice, and finally a summary of what action has been taken, and why. My client, as he has now become, knows he has been dealing with a professional, and as the years go by and his memories of our original meeting fade, he can refer back to my report to remind himself of what action was taken and his circumstances at the time which were relevant to the decisions made.

There is no reason at all why a copy of your report should not be made available, if appropriate, to your client's solicitor and accountant. After all, you may well have spoken to them during your work on the client's affairs, and they are part of his professional advisory team. Better to have them on your side than as adversaries!

CLOSING THE SALE

One of the 10 steps in the LIMRA book is entitled 'Closing the Sale' and much has been written about the subject. In my experience sales do not have to be closed if you follow the two stage process of factfinding, designing and presenting solutions. As a result of your work, your client will have become aware of both the existence and the extent of his problems. You have shown him solutions and it is entirely a matter for him to decide whether or not he wishes to buy them. Following the Broad Concept you have encouraged your prospect to paint his own word pictures, and either they disturb him or they don't. If you have to 'sell' you have a policyholder. If he 'buys' you have a client for life. The better your presentation, the more likely that is to happen.

MATURE SIMPLICITY

Stage 3 of an agent's development has been described as mature simplicity. No longer do you need to demonstrate how clever you are, it's down to basics. "Selling is 90 per cent knowledge of people, and 10 per cent technical knowledge, but you must have 100 per cent of the 10 per cent". Very true, but what you do not need is to put the 100 per cent into written presentations. Keep it supremely simple — the 'KISS' formula should be the order of the day — particularly in any reports you prepare. They will be much more effective and you can always back them up with technical explanations when you get 'face to face'.

CHAPTER 6

Keeping Good Records

TRADITIONALLY SALESMEN have a reputation for being very bad at administration. Probably one of the first things to attract them to the job was the opportunity to get away from what they saw as the drudgery of sitting behind a desk pumping paper. Having escaped, the last thing they want to do is become office bound, for it is far more fun to be out and about in the field hunting for business.

Paradoxically, I have found almost without exception, that the top producers have very effective administration and, in particular, keep outstanding records.

An efficient record keeping system is essential to any enterprise. Every hour an aeroplane flies has to be logged, as does all work carried out on it. There are even separate log books for individual components such as the airframe and the engine. Details of all spare parts and replacements are logged and, of course, routine servicing and maintenance.

It is important to be clear about the purpose of these records. They are not simply an historical catalogue of what has taken place. As such they would be of little use except to historians. What they do provide is a very clear picture of the condition of the aeroplane and its efficiency. The aircraft's condition can be measured against known criteria, and related to the work which has been done on it.

We need to keep records for precisely the same reason. They are only worth keeping if they provide lessons for the future; records for records' sake are useless!

For us there are two types of records — past and present. The past shows what has been done and, therefore, could be done again — or what we need to do in order to achieve our goals in the future. Our present records show us whether we are doing it.

My nephew, a doctor, was telling me one Monday how busy he had been over the weekend in the hospital where he worked. Nearly 40 emergency cases had to be dealt with. I asked what were the first things he did when examining a patient. “Check the vital signs”, he said. “Pulse, heart, blood pressure, reflexes. Then you have an immediate idea of the state of the patient’s health.”

The records we have of what we have done in the past are our vital statistics — know them and check them regularly.

How many approaches do you have to make to get an appointment? What is your appointments to meetings ratio? How many meetings generate full factfinds? What is your closing ratio of sales to factfinds? These are the basic vital statistics for the life assurance agent. Certainly they are historical, but they are also prophetic. If you go on doing what you have been doing in the past, you know precisely what your results will be in the future. Unless *you* change *they* won’t!

What is the value of each appointment, meeting, factfind, sale? What is your time worth per hour? Even more important, what is the value of each hour spent in front of a prospect? Research shows the average salesperson spends only 16 per cent of his time face to face with prospects or clients. When you are aware of that statistic you begin to have a real appreciation of your true value.

Knowing these statistics is absolutely crucial when you are getting down to goal setting and objectives. They are an essential part of the first step in all future planning, and unless you have kept records you won’t know where to start.

Let us say you want to increase your business in the next 12 months by 20 per cent. How do you plan to do it? “Have more appointments”, may well be your answer. That’s fine, but it does not go far enough. How many more do you need? “I intend to increase my case size”. Fine; from what to what, and how? Simply making a statement will not make it happen. You need to know your starting point and from that what you need to do to achieve your objectives.

Incidentally, probably the most effective way of increasing production from one year to the next is to improve your ‘meetings per sale’ ratio.

TODAY’S RECORDS

Acknowledging that salespeople are by nature not good at paperwork, any record system you use has to be simplicity personified! If it isn’t you won’t maintain it! Could you manage 15 minutes a week on basic record keeping? That is all it should take, provided you have the right system.

You can, of course, design your own. I have told you the basic information you need, and a quick trip to the local stationers will produce a suitable A4 book. A page a day, sub-divided into approaches, appointments, meetings, factfinds, sales and value; and use a tick system. At the end of the day total the ticks and spend a few minutes on Saturday morning collating and analysing them.

If you want to get more technical, then back up this incredibly simple system with BAFLAC (the Business Analysis Folio for Life Insurance Consultants)*. I have been using it for many years; it is truly fascinating and educational for me to compare my performance year on year under the various headings. The BAFLAC system takes record keeping all the stages beyond basic statistics and provides what I believe to be crucial additional information. For example, it includes analysis of the source of business and the objectives. (The 'source' and 'objectives' sections are produced at the end of this chapter.)

I am able to see exactly how much business I have had from seminars, existing clients, referrals, advertising and professional advisers. Over the years I have been keeping these records, the percentages have changed quite dramatically, and I have been able to pinpoint areas of strengths and weaknesses. For instance, there was a time when I was putting considerable effort into seminars, but my statistics showed the results were poor. Something was going wrong; the concept of seminars was correct but, clearly, I was not going about them the right way. I made changes and could plot the improvement in performance by using the BAFLAC system.

An analysis of the type of business being written is equally important. Again over the years I have seen a change in the pattern. Initially, the emphasis was heavily on protection, but now it has swung over towards pensions. Party this is because a large percentage of my business comes from existing clients for whom I arranged substantial life assurance when they first came into my practice. Interestingly, I know that my average case for an existing client produces about one third less in gross income terms than is generated by a new client; when the significance of this statistic became obvious, I went back into the 'client acquisition' mode in order to improve my productivity.

I find these statistics extremely encouraging. All salesmen get into

* Published by Prestwood Enterprises, Beauchamp House, Prestwood, Stourbridge DY7 5AS.

a slump from time to time when, whatever you do, nothing ever seems to go right. When that happens to me I simply look back over my records and know that provided I go on doing what I have done in the past, everything will come right. The law of averages always works.

This form of record keeping is a perfect example of the Broad Concept. My present records show me where I am now. My objectives tell me where I want to be, and the alternatives are to be found in the statistics of what I have done in the past. It is not difficult then for me to work out the best alternatives for improvement in the future.

NEW BUSINESS ACTIVITY

Statistical records deal with one part of our business. There is another set equally vital, and fortunately just as easy to maintain.

In Chapter 1, I referred briefly to my applications register; it is time to share with you in more detail the system I designed for myself in 1965, and use to this day.

Item One — a One Card System. The heart is a filing box containing two sets of index cards; '1 to 31' and 'January to December'. A 6 x 4 ins card is opened for every prospect. On it I keep basic details — name, address, telephone number, source of introduction and any other relevant information. The card is filed in the appropriate one to one section on the date the prospect is to be contacted. If an appointment is made on the first contact, the card is re-filed in the appropriate date.

Of course, many initial contacts will not produce an immediate appointment. In such circumstances it is crucial to identify and agree a follow-up date. For example, "Would you have any objection if I called you again in three months to see if your circumstances have changed?" Alternatively, I might find out a prospect's birthday, the time of his next salary review or, if it is a corporate prospect, the company year end. The card is then re-filed in the appropriate month for the follow-up.

In the third week of every month all the cards for the following month are extracted and re-filed in the '1 to 31' section on the dates on which follow-up action is to be taken. Each day the cards in the appropriate date are extracted and dealt with. The bottom half of the card is used to note brief details of every contact and conversation with the prospect.

I have experimented with just about every system man ever

created; without doubt this is the most simple and highly effective there is. Within a few short weeks of introducing it into your practice it could contain several hundred names. To start off, go through everyone in your prospect files and create a separate card. Get into the discipline of looking through your monthly box on the first Monday of the third week of every month, and the '1 to 31' section the night before.

It is very rare for a prospect card to be destroyed; it is simply carried forward from one section to the next until, ultimately, the prospect becomes a client or dies! The key to the whole system, however, is the identification of a specific follow-up date or opportunity. The essential feature is that the follow-up date must take place exactly on the date pre-selected.

Routine, easy to operate, compact and inexpensive to set-up, the system gives great comfort to the agent when he sees the number of cards building up, because he knows it is his gold mine for the future. Within a year you can have 50 cards a month to deal with before you start any new prospecting. I use the same card system for client follow-up — more about that in the next chapter on Servicing.

WORK IN PROGRESS

All good businesses have a work in progress record — a simple summary of all current case work. Why should we be any different? I make a list of the cases I am reasonably confident I will secure in the next 30 days. I 'rate' my anticipated chances of success with the 'most likely cases' top of the list.

I want a minimum of 30 cases on this list at any one time. I draw a line across it when I make out the list so that I know what names are added during the month. Every time I make a sale I 'highlight' the case which I find motivational.

I have a second sheet opened for the following month for cases which get carried forward.

I look at this sheet constantly — by which I mean several times a day. I am no different from any other agent. Sometimes people don't buy from me! When I know there is a need, I am constantly asking myself, "What can I say to this person to help him make up his mind?" Looking at the list on a regular basis means my prospects are always in the forefront of my mind.

Of course you need a diary where you keep a note of your

appointments, first and second interviews, service calls, administration work and so on. I use a system of coloured dots to identify different activities — red for first interview, blue for second. Green stands for servicing, and yellow for office work. By using such a system you can, at a glance, see a profile of your daily activity which will focus your attention on better time management.

I also maintain a register in which I record every application I secure. This is the very heart of my business; by using it I know which cases have been completed, which are still 'in the pipeline'. Looking back over previous years I find it a very useful re-canvassing tool, and it helps me to make comparisons between one year and the next. These are the headings for my Applications Register:

No	Date	Name	New or Cl	Type	Prem A/S	Int Comm	Ren Comm	Issued

When cases go in-force they are entered into the completions section of my BAFLAC, within which there is a page for each week.

On Saturday morning I spend no more than 15 minutes working out my current 'vital signs' and comparing them with my objectives. Now I know precisely what I have to do in the remaining weeks of the year.

The 'analysis of business year to date by objectives and source' shows me whether the marketing initiatives undertaken are being effective — a classic example of an historical records system providing crucial on-going management information, essential for long term business planning.

The system I have described really is simple, but its success depends on one vital factor. You have to discipline yourself to use it. Salespeople tend not to be amongst the 25 per cent of the population who are mainly analytically minded. We are more likely to be expressive or drivers, and a few of us amiables; none of these three categories are particularly good at paperwork. The driver can't see the point of it, the expressive is bored by it and the amiable simply wants to be friendly with people. Nevertheless, each of us has at least a small portion of 'analytical' and all you have to do is harness it for just 15 minutes and it could turn out to be the most valuable quarter of an hour of your entire week.

Analysis of Completed Cases by Source of Business — Year to Date				
Source of Business	*No of Cases*	*% of Total*	*Initial Comm*	*% of Total*
Intros from Prof Advisers				
Other referred leads				
Seminars				
Existing clients				
Advertising				
Direct mail replies				
Cold approaches				
TOTAL				

Analysis of Completed Cases by Objectives — Year to Date				
Objective *No of Cases*	*Total Int Comm*	*Av Comm per Case*	*MDRT Credit*	*Total Rnl Comm*
Childpols				
IHT				
Education				
Fam Prot/PHI				
Investment				
Keyman				
Mortgage				
Pensions				
TOTAL				

CHAPTER 7

Service What You Sell

HOW OFTEN HAVE WE had the experience of carrying out a full factfind with a prospective client to discover he has existing policies with four or five different insurance companies? Frequently, I expect, and what does it tell you? Quite simply, that the agent who arranged those previous policies has been both guilty and short sighted. Guilty, because clearly he has failed to provide what his clients were entitled to expect — after sales service. Short sighted because as a result when the client needed additional coverage, he had bought elsewhere.

We are told insurance is a service industry; yet in any thesis on selling, service always appears as the last step in the sales process. I believe it is frequently the first step leading to the second sale, and for this reason my mental image of the sales process is of a circle, because it is very hard to say where one step stops and another starts.

When does service begin? In most cases before the first sale is actually made. For example, gathering together all the information about a client's existing insurance portfolio and getting the valuations for him is providing service, and you would do that before making your presentation.

At times there can be a long delay between the provision of service and the first sale. I have a magnificent photograph on the wall of my office of a Bristol Gamecock aeroplane to remind me of this fact. One Saturday morning a man and his wife walked into my office and asked if I was available to give them advice on some existing insurance policies. We talked for about two hours because the man was an RAF squadron leader and a test pilot. He happened to have with him a portfolio of photographs including some showing his test flying the Canberra jet bomber. Amazingly, I had stood on the runway at RAF Marham some years previously and, without realising it, actually watched this man demonstrating that same aircraft.

We didn't do any business on the day, and I declined his offer of a fee. I had simply enjoyed meeting with him and that was sufficient.

Three weeks later, a parcel arrived containing a framed copy of the Bristol Gamecock aeroplane I had so much admired. It was his way of paying me for the time I had spent with him.

Some three years later, that same squadron leader, now retired, walked into my office once again, and this time we did some business together. The photograph serves to remind me that you never know when you are planting seed which one day will enable you to reap a harvest.

The last two decades have seen enormous strides in the development of technology. No self respecting businessman can fail to have his quota of pocket calculators, computerised diaries, word processing machines and electronic memory banks. It makes me wonder how we ever managed in our early days with a loose-leaf rate book, a foolscap pad, an Imperial typewriter and a shorthand typist. I can tell you one thing for certain. In those days there was far more personal contact between the agent and his client, because electronic wizardry was not there to get in the way.

In my experience the public are now turning back to service. Price is less important that the quality of attention they get from their suppliers, whether it be the waitress in the local restaurant or the garage where they buy their petrol, the travel agent to whom they entrust their family holiday or their life insurance agent. Providing an excellent level of service is a way of showing you care for your customer, and that is bound to produce a favourable response.

SAFEGUARDING YOUR FUTURE — AND YOUR CLIENTS

How do you define a client? In my book it is a policyholder to whom you provide a high level of service. It is not sufficient for you to think of him as a client; he has to think that way himself. After all, a number of other people regard him as their client. For example, his building society, bank, solicitor, accountant, doctor and dentist are obvious examples, and certainly the first four may well be able to offer him financial products. What you have to do is ensure that whenever your client thinks about life insurance, pensions and investments, he turns to you rather than some of your competitors.

Be aware that many of these competitors have enormous financial clout. They can mount regular, sophisticated mailing campaigns and because of their size are sometimes able to offer exclusive terms not otherwise available to you.

When I started my broking business in 1965 I recall clearly saying to my secretary: "There are a lot of other people in the industry who are able to market exactly the same products as us. What we are going to do is try to provide a better level of service because that will set us apart from our competitors." I have always tried to do just that and it seems to work.

The first justification for it is in order to conserve what you have. A well sold, well serviced policy will not lapse, and frankly there is no point whatsoever in attempting to increase your production by 20 per cent this year, if a similar percentage of last year's business is dropping off the books.

Second, service will ultimately lead to further sales and, of course, recommendations and introductions. Within 12 to 24 months a new agent should expect to see something approaching 50 per cent of his production each year coming from his existing client bank.

Currently around 76 per cent of my production is coming from existing clients, and my lapse rate is below 5 per cent. These figures have only been achieved by very hard work and total commitment to the concept of service. Indeed, when I take on a new client I say to him, "I plan to service you to death." Yes, there is meant to be a double meaning and they usually realise it. In all probability they don't believe it at first, because they have undoubtedly had experience with other agents which has shown this is not normally the case. I set out to prove to them I mean what I say, and I basically do it by keeping in touch on a regular basis.

That does not simply mean I am always trying to get them to buy more products, although obviously that comes into it. After all, if they have needs, it's down to me to ensure they realise it, and give them an opportunity to consider whether or not to do something about it. What I really want to do is make sure they never forget me, and this can only be achieved by introducing a disciplined servicing system.

A SIMPLE SYSTEM THAT WORKS

All clients do not need the same level of service. Indeed there are some that might be resentful if you made contact with them too often during the course of a year, whereas there are others who would feel neglected if you only contacted them once. What you need to do, therefore, is to categorise your clients and design your servicing processes. As outlined in Chapter 2, I believe three categories are sufficient:

CATEGORY A. Ideal clients. I have ruthlessly analysed my client bank and find that only 16 per cent fall into this category. This is my criteria:

1. Entrepreneurially minded men and women.
2. High networth (or potential).
3. In a position of influence.
4. Decision makers.
5. Growth orientated.
6. Favourably responsive to my suggestions in a businesslike manner.
7. Serving them has been profitable to me.
8. I am comfortable working with them.
9. They fit into my chosen market.
10. They are individuals to whom I believe I can make a significant contribution in terms of 'added value'.
11. They are a valuable source of introductions and recommendations.

These clients are clearly my most valuable asset, and are worthy of the highest level of service I am able to provide. They just about confirm the well know 80-20 Perato rule because certainly around 80 per cent of my business comes from close on 20 per cent of my client bank.

It is important to tell your ideal client he falls into that category, and I use this letter:

> "I have introduced what I call the Ideal Client system into my financial practice, and measured my existing clients against the standards I have established.
>
> Approximately 16 per cent meet the exacting criteria, and I am very pleased to say that you are amongst them.
>
> I want to explain the special services I shall be offering you in the future, and to show you how I propose to 'add value' to your business; I will be telephoning shortly to arrange a meeting."

Each month I select a number of my category A clients to receive this letter, and when we meet I give them a copy of my criteria. I then explain the services which I intend to provide:

1. An in-depth analysis of their business and personal financial programme each year.

2. The preparation of a financial review, including valuations of all existing contracts.
3. An annual up-date.
4. An opportunity to meet other ideal clients whether at formal dinners or a small select seminar.
5. An executive counselling service.
6. Six editions of a financial bulletin each year.
7. A quarterly investment bulletin.
8. A birthday card.

In addition I review my list of Category A clients after any changes in legislation which may impact upon business, and in particular the Budget. The launch of new products would also prompt a review.

These are clients whose files hardly ever get out of my outstanding drawer. There is always something happening with their business, and I clearly need to know about it.

CATEGORY B. This group comprises clients who I believe have potential but who do not yet qualify for Category A classification. They may well at some time in the future. Here is my servicing procedure for this group:
1. A personal letter goes to each of them during their birthday month. This draws attention to the various services I offer and the ways in which I might be able to help them. It offers a personal visit, and includes a reply card.
2. I select a number of clients who I have reason to believe might well respond favourably to a call from me, and these I telephone — a number of appointments will result.
3. They will receive six financial bulletins from me during the year.
4. Each will receive a birthday card.
5. They will also have two investment bulletins — one in January, the other in July.

CATEGORY C. The balance of my clients. They comprise annuitants, holders of home income plans, elderly investors and the like who almost certainly will have no further servicing needs from me.

However, you can never tell, and I certainly would not neglect them. They will certainly get birthday greetings and I would include 'a request for meeting' card in case they feel they need to see me. They will also have at least one, and possibly two financial bulletins.

It is my practice to include a number of my clients on the mailing list for the investment and inheritance tax seminars I hold on a regular basis. I don't mind if there's no business to do with them, it is nice just to have them there and to provide some hospitality. Of course, I am not unmindful of the fact they may well talk to some of the other delegates and mention the work I have done for them.

USE OF A CHECKLIST

Few are blessed with perfect memories and when something really important is involved it is surely better to have some help. Take a lead from the aviation industry and follow their example. No matter how many times they have flown, an aircrew always uses a number of checklists to monitor their actions. We should do the same.

At the point of sale and in preparing for a review meeting we need a checklist to ensure we do not forget any important matters when we are with our client. This is the one I use:

	DATE DISCUSSED	*ACTION*
Income for the family		
Loan/mortgage cover		
Disability cover		
Retirement provision		
Wife insurance		
Child policies		
School fees		
Savings		
Investment		
Parents/in-laws/HIP/investment		
Private medical schemes		
Grandchildren/godchildren		
Inheritance tax		
Partnership		
Keyman		
Loan account		
Capital account		
Share protection		
Loans		
Share option		
Introductions/recommendations		

The headings are obvious. You keep a copy inside each client's file and up-date it everytime you meet with him. I consider it to be part of the factfind and helps to ensure that the advice I give is not only the best of which I am capable, but that it is complete. It is all too easy to overlook an item but the checklist ensures this does not happen.

In preparing for a client review meeting I will go through the checklist looking in particular for gaps — things that we have not done. If I believe the client has a need in one of those areas I will take pre-prepared illustrations with me so that we have something specific to discuss.

THE USE OF AGENDAS

The secret of any well run meeting is to have a carefully prepared agenda. If you are calling a meeting it is your responsibility to set the agenda. Having decided what you want to talk about, why not tell your client as well and send him a copy. 'Any other business' will allow him to bring up subjects he particularly wants to include in your next discussion.

Agendas add a degree of formality to meetings and that is how it should be; after all, it is a business meeting. They ensure you stay on track and become the basis of the records you create of each meeting.

NEGLECT AT YOUR PERIL

Good servicing solves a major part of your prospecting problem for all time. The right to service your clients is an honour and a privilege which was conferred upon you when they became policyholders. You must not expect your client's loyalty as a right. It has to be earned, and if you do not work at it somebody else just might sell your client his next policy.

CHAPTER 8

Managing Your Time

THE MORE SUCCESSFUL you get, the more time you need, and the less you seem to have. Strangely enough, there is an old saying — if you want to get something done, ask a busy man! The paradox is, no one has enough time yet everyone has all the time there is.

"Doesn't the time fly." "There never seems to be enough hours in the day." "I don't know where the time has gone." "I didn't have enough time to do it." "I ran out of time." I wonder how often we use one or all those phrases in the course of a day. Frequently I suspect, and yet they are all meaningless. After all, time goes at the same pace; the second hand of your watch doesn't suddenly speed up, unless of course, there is something wrong with it. It just feels as though it does!

Achievers in all walks of life always seem to have enough time. Not content with running a successful business you find they are involved in charities, committee work, local politics, and even squeeze in the occasional game of golf.

Clearly, they have found the secret of managing their time and one wonders which came first. Was it managing their time which helped to make them successful; or finding themselves on the way to success, did they then have to put some disciplines into the way they ran their lives?

Time is, in fact, the biggest problem. The majority of people either have too little or too much. When your work load increases you have too little. When you are new in the business, with only two or three appointments in a week, you have too much. Strangely enough, the solutions to both situations are virtually identical.

The key words are plan and control, but you cannot begin to do either until you carry out a personal factfind. Back to the Broad Concept; where are you now?

A TIME LOG

You probably think you have a good idea of where your time goes, but almost certainly you will be wrong. The only way you can find out is to run a time log on your own activity over a minimum period of a week and, ideally, four weeks. This is how you do it:

Buy some sheets of graph paper and across the top mark off hourly divisions and divide each hour into four 15 minute segments. On the lefthand side have the days of the week (see illustration).

Take four different coloured crayons to represent your main activities. I use red to denote face to face time with prospects or clients. Green stands for travel, yellow for time spent in the office, and black for personal activities — getting your hair cut, playing golf or whatever you do when you're supposed to be working!

As the day progresses you colour each 15 minute square with the appropriate crayon and begin to build-up a really accurate picture of where you spend and waste your time.

After two or three days you will find an overwhelming tendency to cheat. Knowing your most valuable time is face to face with clients you

TIME PLANNING STUDY

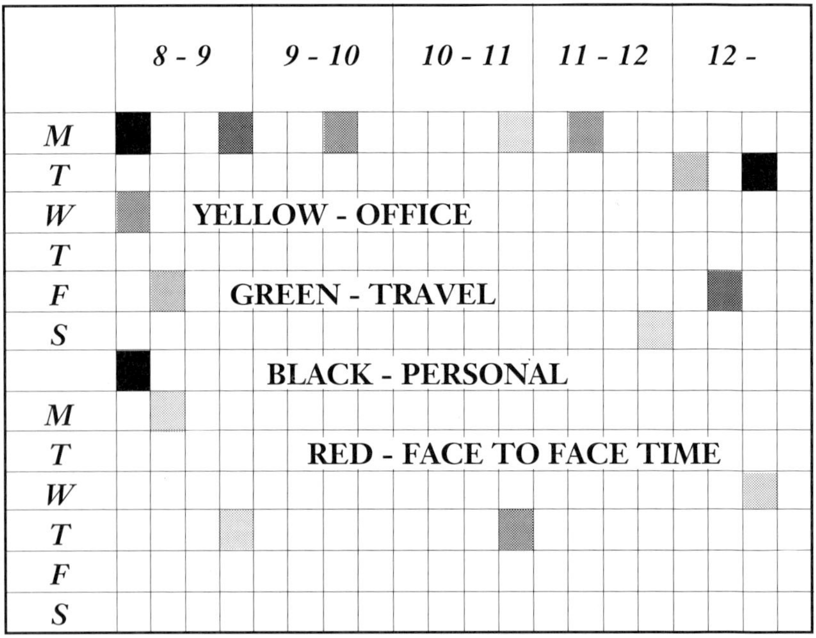

will be horrified at how few red squares you have. "I suppose speaking to a prospect on the telephone is the same as having a face to face meeting", is what you are likely to say to yourself. It is not! The only person you will be deceiving is yourself if you adopt that kind of attitude.

Interestingly enough, your time log will not give you a truly accurate picture of the way you have been spending your time in the past, because the moment you start using it, your time planning improves. You become more aware, and subconsciously begin to make changes.

When I carried out my first time log study I found only 16 per cent of my time was spent face to face with clients or prospects. Twenty per cent went on travel, 10 per cent on personal items, and a staggering 54 per cent in the office. As you may imagine I was very unhappy and some changes had to be made.

You may have your own reasons for wanting to 'create' more time. Perhaps you do not want to increase your production but simply spend more time on your personal life, or with your family. It really does not matter what your motives are, running the time log is your starting point.

In my case, at the time I wanted to increase my production and that clearly meant spending more time in front of prospects and clients. The hours had to come from my other activities and so step two of the time log was to find out exactly what I was doing in the 54 per cent of time I spent in the office, and to have a hard look at the travel time.

Most salespeople seem to drive between 15,000 and 20,000 miles a year. Assuming your average speed is 40 miles an hour (which, frankly, is on the high side) you spend 500 hours behind the wheel of your car. On the basis of a 40 hour week that is 12 1/2 weeks, or to put in another way, 62 1/2 days. Assuming you average three appointments a day, your closing ratio is 1 in 3 and your average gross sale £300, every hour spent in your car costs you £37.50 — on top, of course, of depreciation, petrol and other running costs. Those statistics should surely encourage you to look very seriously at your travel item. To quote a well know phrase or saying, "Is your journey really necessary?"

What can you do to improve? The most obvious way is to get prospects and clients to come into the office to see you. The legendary John Savage of Toledo, Ohio, speaking at a convention in London many years ago, claimed he did virtually all of his business in his office. Somebody in the audience said, "John, can you tell us how you get people to come to your office?" His answer was simplicity personified: "I ask them!" Next time you are making appointments on the telephone, why not try it? You may be surprised at the results.

Do you use the telephone as often and as efficiently as you could? Many times we make visits to clients when a telephone call or letter would have done just as well. It is nice to jump in the car on the slightest pretext, convincing yourself it is vital for you to take that direct debit to get your client's signature. Remember £37.50 per hour!

Do you plan your calls on a geographic basis? I learned this lesson in my days as a life inspector, covering all of Suffolk and a substantial part of Essex. I divided my 'patch' into five areas, allocated them days of the week, and that was the only time I was to be found there. This had the added advantage of people getting to know when to expect me and setting up appointments on my behalf. Often I would conduct my meetings in a local hotel, so again people were coming to see me.

When you do have to travel in your car, turn the hours to advantage by listening to motivational or technical cassettes. There are plenty around and it keeps your mind tuned into business. At least it gives you some profit from what would otherwise be an expensive experience.

OFFICE TIME

You can waste a great deal of time in the office! It's an ideal place to chat over a cup of coffee, read the local paper, study the latest head office or insurance company circular, and generally find anything to do apart from talking to clients!

When I first became interested in time management, I devised the concept of 'prime time' and 'down time'. Prime time I defined as any hours when I could actually hope to be sitting in front of prospects or clients. Down times were obviously hours when I could not see them for one reason or another. I made a rule I would not deal with 'down time activity' during prime time. Down time activity included such items as reading company circulars, bulletins, new product particulars, and financial magazines. Nowadays I include on my list playing with my computer — a very insidious time waster if you are not careful! I would commend the concept of prime time and down time to you.

Back to the time log. You will find as I did, that more than half your time is actually spent in the office. The next step is to analyse just what you are doing. In fact, this has probably been done for you because some years ago the Million Dollar Round Table sent out a survey on time wasting to its membership, and believe it or not, the first dozen or so items all related to office activities. Your list, and the solutions will almost certainly be the same. This is what MDRT found:

Telephone calls. This was the number one time waster. The telephone has the ability to pierce through almost every defence if we allow it to do so. Indeed, most businessmen encourage it, because the ring of the telephone carries with it a sense of urgency and you simply feel you have to pick up the receiver.

It is not simply the time you spend dealing with the call itself. If you are involved in some casework study for a client, your train of thought has been disrupted and you have to go back to the beginning. Before you even get back to where you were the telephone rings again, and so it goes on. What are the solutions?

First of all, if possible, have your calls screened by your telephonist, receptionist, personal assistant or secretary. Brief them thoroughly on what is important and what is not, and they will then use their judgement in either putting the call through to you or arranging for you to call back.

If you have staff, delegate as much responsibility back to them as you can in dealing with clients. After a while you will actually find your clients begin to ask for your staff rather than you, because in most cases they get faster answers. Remember they are busy people too, yet courtesy dictates when they come through to you personally, there has to be an element of social chat before you get down to business.

It is a good idea to have a quiet hour (or even longer) if you are particularly busy. Take no calls at all during that time. You really will have to exercise great discipline on this one, but just remember if you were on holiday or away from the office for any other reason you would not be there to take the call anyway. Make sure the callers know what time you will return their call, because again you are helping their time planning.

Group your own telephone calls. I make a list of the calls I have to make, complete with the telephone numbers, allocate an hour or so to the exercise, make myself unavailable to any other calls, no visitors, and simply do not put down the receiver until I have finished.

Drop in visitors. It is all very well to have an open door policy but it does encourage 'drop in' visitors. They drop in when it is convenient to them, not necessarily convenient to you.

The first thing you can do, of course, is close your door from time to time and put a 'Do not disturb' notice on it. When it is open and people drop in, ask them how much of your time they need, and if it isn't convenient then, make an appointment. After all, it is almost certainly a business meeting and these are best done on an appointment basis.

Tell your secretary (if you are fortunate to have one) how long you want a meeting to last. At the pre-arranged finishing time she 'interrupts', reminding you of your next meeting.

If, despite all this, someone gets through the screen you have thrown up around you, come around to the front of your desk and stay on your feet. Meetings conducted standing up have a wonderful way of being shorter than those when you are sitting down!

Meetings. "Let's have a meeting to discuss it", is a phrase you hear too frequently nowadays and you know most of them will go on too long and not come to any decisions. The answer is always to have an agenda for a formal meeting, and a timetable clearly stated. You must start on time even if some of the participants are not present. I do not believe in penalising those who take the trouble to arrive on time, and rewarding those who come late!

If you are in charge of the meeting, it is your responsibility to ensure people stick to the agenda, to the subject under discussion, and to the previously agreed timescale. Constantly throughout the meeting you remind people of the time the meeting is due to close, and when that time arrives you close it.

There is a knack in preparing an agenda. Most people get it wrong. They put the simple matters at the beginning and the complicated ones, where much discussion is bound to take place, at the end. Do it the other way round. Important matters come first to ensure there is adequate time for them to be dealt with. If there is any time left you can begin to deal with the more routine matters.

Crisis! I call this one fire fighting. A crisis develops and the overwhelming urge is to drop everything else and deal with it.

First of all you have to realise that it is more likely to be someone else's crisis than it is yours, and you just get dragged into it. Only deal immediately with your own fire fighting problems. Careful planning in advance reduces the likelihood of a crisis developing, but when it does do not over-react. Put it in its place and finish what you are doing first. A wise man builds some 'cushion' time into every day for just that purpose.

Lack of objectives, priorities and deadlines. This is part of planning. If you find that all too frequently you are not ready for a meeting or client visit, you are not planning. Ben Feldman says he spends hours getting ready to get ready. An hour spent on planning is worth five hours in the field, and if you can discipline yourself to do so, this particular time-trap will no longer be a problem for you.

Cluttered desk. Some people seem to work well surrounded by piles of paper, or they think they do. In fact, the opposite is probably true. It is not just that you cannot find items, but simply having the paper there inhibits good working practices.

The solution is very simple indeed. Get more desks or use the floor! Try to keep on your desk only what you are working on and move everything else out of the way.

Attempting too much. A common fault I fear, and probably my biggest problem! Take on less, and wherever possible delegate more. If you do not have someone to delegate to, maybe now is the time to employ one.

Inability to say no. Closely related to attempting too much, of course. Our ego is massaged when people ask us to do something, and we say yes without thinking. We are flattered and also we don't want to hurt people's feelings by saying no. Next time you get a request to do something, respond by saying, "I am not quite sure what my commitments are at the moment. Could I call you back in a few moments when I have had a chance to look at my diary?" Then you can make a decision without feeling pressure and it's more likely to be the right one.

Lack of controls. This is what happens when you have no systems or the ones you have are inadequate. You just stagger from one situation to another. If you get to the right destination it's more by accident than design! If you are not good at controlling systems yourself, delegate the responsibility to someone else.

Indecision. The reason we don't make decisions is because of the fear of being wrong. We will never be right all the time, but as long as your batting average is 1 in 3 or better, you don't really have a problem.

SOME USEFUL TIPS

I became interested in time management as a result of attending my first MDRT meeting in Montreal. Since then I have developed my own techniques and solutions to assist my personal time management and you may find some of them helpful:

Appointments with self. From time to time make an appointment with yourself. Put your own name in the diary and allocate an hour or more to a particular job. You become your own client and that period of time is inviolate.

Dummy appointments. When my time management shows signs of getting somewhat out of control, my secretary is not above putting a dummy appointment in my diary — although I don't know it's one. She will tell me a little white lie, and it is not until a few minutes before the 'client' is due to come in that she will confess it's a dummy and she has 'bought' me an extra hour.

Cancelled appointments. I actually love cancelled appointments! I thank people, which they find a little surprising. However, when I explain it gives me an unscheduled hour which I can always use to advantage, they feel good about it.

Deal with mail. Dictate your mail on a pocket memo machine as you go along. It only takes a minute or two, and is much better than leaving it until the following morning. In any event, always make sure you have dictated all your mail the night before.

The concept of a dream week. Plan your 'dream week'. In it you will probably have 16 appointments and time set aside for marketing activities, some personal time, and hours with your family. You will never achieve your dream week, but having a plan means you will get a lot nearer to it than you would without.

A Saturday drawer. It is rare for me to see clients on a Saturday so it is designated down time. All correspondence, magazines, circulars and so on that come in during the week are consigned to the drawer in my desk which is called the Saturday Drawer. Monday to Friday I am putting things into it; Saturday morning I take it out in a heap and just go through it — one piece of paper at a time.

Much of it I find I don't even need to read, and the rest I deal with much more efficiently than I would if I tried to handle it during prime time. I allocate a maximum of two hours to this task and anything that has not been dealt with goes back into the drawer for another seven days.

Handle paper once. Only I suppose that isn't quite right because my 'down' material is handled when I receive it, and again on Saturday morning. What I try not to do is move things from one pile to another until what was routine becomes urgent and important. Decide its status, allocate it to the right unit of time and then deal with it.

The A4 sheet. I plan my entire day around at A4 sheet. I divide it into four squares; in one I list telephone calls that I have to make, and in another things I have to do.

The third square is reserved for matters I want to discuss with my staff, and in the fourth I jot down any marketing and planning ideas I want to consider. These will be put into my main planning strategy, probably on a Saturday morning.

A new sheet for every day, and the first two sections are always completed 'the night before'. Anything left undone is simply carried forward.

The mobile phone. There are certain items you acquire which have a major impact upon the quality of life, and certainly the mobile phone comes into this category. It 'lifts the pressure', enabling me to deal with urgent matters in those hours when I have to be in the car or on the train, and I am always in touch with my office. It is worth its weight in gold.

Do a '360'. Despite everything else, from time to time, I feel the pressure and tension which comes from attempting too much, having a cluttered desk, losing sight of my objectives, having my third crisis of the day! When I become aware of this I stop whatever I am doing and carry out a '360'.

I start by the door of my office and spend half an hour or so going completely around everything until I get back to the door again. The piles of papers get sorted out and given priorities, anything not urgent goes into the Saturday drawer, and by the time I have completed my circuit I have my brain back in gear, life under control, and I know precisely what I should be doing next.

Delegate. Most of us are not very good at delegation because we do not think other people are capable of doing the job as well as ourselves. In many instances we are wrong. They can do better than us but, of course, it would hurt our ego to admit it!

To have true control over our time, the ability to delegate is vital. However generous an employer you may be, it is doubtful you are paying your staff anywhere near as much as you earn yourself per hour. Why, therefore, do a job at your rate of pay when you can delegate it to somebody else who will do it just as well (if not better) and cheaper?

After you have run your time log, keep another record of everything you do in a week. On Saturday ask yourself this question about every single item. "Could someone else have done this instead of me?" Do that regularly and you will become, in time, a good delegator.

WOULD YOU LIKE TO FIND AN EXTRA TWO HOURS A DAY?

As those around me will readily admit, my time planning still leaves much to be desired, but I claim to be better than most. However, some while ago, unexpected circumstances meant I needed to find an extra two hours a day and at first sight this was quite a challenge. As it turned out it was much easier than I thought.

I have always been an early starter, and was usually to be found at my desk at 7.30 to 7.45. Getting in at 7 am gained me at least 30 minutes and really was no great effort. Add 30 minutes at the other end of the day by finishing later and I had solved half my problem. What about lunch? Most of us have been brought up to expect an hour to an hour and a quarter for lunchbreak, but is it really necessary? I found allocating certain work to the lunch period and taking it in the office, with sandwiches and a cup of coffee, involved no hardship. I still had a break, yet I turned the lunch hour to my advantage and effectively found a further 60 minutes.

Work it out: two hours a day, five days a week, 46 weeks of the year, is 460 hours, the equivalent of 58 days. Add back just half the time you currently spend on travelling and I have found you 89 days or 712 hours, during which you could have 300 additional appointments.

That may sound too good to be true, but does it really matter? After all, if you only achieve 50 per cent you will have an additional 150 appointments in a year, without actually working any harder. What good time management enables you to do is work smarter, to make the best use of the most precious resource known to man.

As Parkinson's Law says, work does tend to expand to fill the time available. But I would add, only if we let it. If you are busy now, you may well be saying, "I would love to do something about it, but I just don't have the time to spend running a time log." I would put it the other way; you cannot afford not to spend the time doing it if you are determined to take control, rather than be controlled.

CHAPTER 9

Setting Goals

"I *BELIEVE THAT THIS* nation should commit itself to achieve the goal, before this decade is out, of landing a man on the Moon and returning him safely to Earth. No single space project in this area will be more impressive to mankind, or more important for the long-range exploration of space, and none will be so difficult or expensive to accomplish for in a very real sense it will not be one man going to the moon, it will be the entire nation." — John F. Kennedy, 25th May 1961.

That has to be the most exciting, dynamic and motivational goal I have ever come across. No one who heard those words of John F. Kennedy failed to go out that evening and look up to the moon, and picture man walking on it. Man actually walked on the moon on 20th July 1969 but, to my way of thinking, the mission was really accomplished in May 1961 when the goal was established. We all just knew it would happen. It is said, a goal should be within your reach, but not your grasp. Before we even get around to setting goals, we have to decide why they are necessary in the first place. What is their purpose? To truly understand goal setting we have to go back to basics and start with a man called Mazlow, who years ago came up with what he described as man's hierarchy of needs.

He placed them in a pyramid with five different levels. The first level is the basic need to survive within our own environment. You might almost call this the base animal instinct. For the Stone Age man that simply meant food and shelter. Nothing else mattered unless those basic needs were met. It was probably man's first ever goal.

The second level Mazlow described as the need for security. Security is a luxury you can begin to enjoy once you know you have solved the problem of survival. Having done it once you want to feel certain in your mind you can go on doing it over and over again, reducing to a minimum the likelihood of slipping back to level 1.

This is followed by the need to belong. If the first two needs are fundamentally introspective, it is at level 3 that one can first begin to go outside one's own environment and think about sharing with other people.

That brings us to level 4 — status or prestige. According to Mazlow you now want the world at large to see how clever you are!

The fifth level he described as self actualisation, the stage where you feel you are realising your full potential. I am personally not convinced that anybody ever gets to this level but plenty of people think they do.

So those are five needs or goals, and if you turn back now to Kennedy's vision, you can see it really contains all five which is perhaps why it was so powerful. You may notice another interesting fact. Mazlow's five needs are all about personal levels of achievement; there is no reference to business, and yet when we in the life insurance industry talk about goals, the thoughts immediately turn to volume and production.

PERSONAL GOALS

Personal goals are truly the important ones. They express what we want to achieve as human beings during our lifetime. However, it is mainly through what we do in our business life that we create the environment which makes it possible to achieve those vital personal goals. The first stage, therefore, in any goal setting exercise is to look at Mazlow and define what we mean by survival, security, belonging, status and self actualisation.

In financial terms what is your survival level? That has to be the minimum goal you set yourself every year. Fail to achieve that and you will certainly miss the other four. Spend some time thinking about the lifestyle you want to create for your family. This would certainly include such items as private education for your children, going into business on your own, moving to the time when your wife can give up work and so on.

What about your material goals? There is nothing wrong in wanting a bigger house, a luxury car, an expensive holiday, but they all need building into your personal goal structure.

That is where you begin. As time goes by you will add other goals to your personal list, such as community involvement or serving your local community in some form of voluntary work.

BUSINESS GOALS

Once you have done that you can begin to think about your business objectives because as I have explained, you will achieve one through the other. There are three main business goals that we in our industry must consider. Production, cash flow and net asset increase.

Because of the way we are remunerated, production generates our basic income. Currently it is the way we are judged by our peers and our companies and as such it is fundamental to our very being.

Staying with my philosophy of keeping things simple, we need to break a goal down into manageable units. They seem much more achievable.

You divide your annual goal by 46 which is the average number of weeks you will work. The result gives you weekly targets and you can divide it again by five to show what you need to produce every working day of the week. Hopefully, you know your case size from records you have been keeping, can calculate how many cases you need to produce, and from your basic ratios the number of sales meetings you must maintain. These are sub goals and, clearly, just as important.

However, production in itself is not enough. I have known people qualify for the Million Dollar Round Table by producing, say, £40,000 of first year commission, only to find that not only can they not afford to attend the Annual Meeting in the USA but they are fast approaching bankruptcy. This is because cash flow is so vital to survival. Our bills come in on a monthly basis and our income has to be sufficient to match them.

In my early days of broking I devised my own cash flow system which was incredibly crude, but remarkably effective. It comprised a register with 24 sheets in it; on each page I entered every policy upon which I was going to get commission that month. If I produced a policy in January I would enter one twenty fourth or, if appropriate, one twelfth of the commission on the following pages so that I knew precisely what I had coming in. It also gave me a good check on whether insurance companies' records were as good as mine!

Nowadays, you can get a computer programme that does it for you, and I do not see how you can truly plan your business without it. It should be part of your own projected income and expenditure cash flow budget, prepared at 1st January, every year. You can show your known expenditure on a month by month basis and your certain income. The deficiency of one to the other is your basic needs goal for the year. Anything over and above that is your wants goal.

The third goal should be an increase in your net asset value. This is your true bottom line. Each and everyone of us is an individual business, and as such we need a balance sheet and a profit and loss account. In this respect we are no different from the largest public limited company. It is not sufficient simply to concern ourselves with profit and loss. Balance sheet assets are just as important.

STANDARDS

Having set your goals, you can now set your standards, which many people think are one and the same — they are not.

The first standard is the number of new clients you feel you are capable of taking on and adequately servicing each year. The number will depend on the market in which you operate. If your clients are mainly from the domestic market you might be looking for somewhere between 50 and 100 each year. Should you be working exclusively in the corporate market, one a month might be as many as you could adequately handle.

The second standard is your own value per hour. You must know what it is and ensure that it does not fall. We should always know our value and be sure we never really undersell ourselves. If you put a realistic value per hour upon your time, it will encourage you to continually upgrade your prospecting.

The third standard is persistency of business. One of my earliest jobs in the life insurance industry was to chase non-renewals. My manager's philosophy was put quite simply: "Clark, there is no point in me chasing the inspectors to produce more new business if we are losing significant levels through lapses. It would be like pushing new applications into a sack which has a hole in the bottom." There are times when a case will lapse through no fault of ours at all, but this is rare. A lapse rate of no more than 10 per cent should be considered standard.

THE ACHIEVEMENT OF GOALS

Goals are transient items. Once you achieve them the excitement has gone. It is rather like the bubbles in a glass of champagne. Leave the glass for a few minutes and the wine goes flat and is no longer palatable.

Failure, though, lasts. If you think back through your life to times when you succeeded at what was, at the time, a very exciting goal, it is hard to recapture the emotion. When you focus on failures, you can still feel the pain.

One of my clients is a renowned artist and I asked him how he could possibly bring himself to part with the magnificent pictures he painted. "No problem, Ken. Whilst I am involved in painting the picture it's very exciting and I can't get to finish it quickly enough. When I finally put the last brushmark on the canvas and sign my name, there is a feeling of anti-climax. I have achieved my goal and provided I take a photograph of it, I don't mind what happens."

So it is for us. Each year we will create our own new records and for a while they will be seen by everybody like a vapour trail in the sky. Then they fade, leaving just a memory. The chase starts all over again.

SHORT TERM INSPIRATION

Achieving goals is itself motivational! We can turn this phenomenon to advantage by setting a series of support goals during the year. As we achieve each one we feel a winner and before the euphoria of success passes into history wc can be into the excitement of the next one.

For example, how about writing a case every day for a month, and having achieved it do it again just to show it wasn't luck?
Here are a few others:

- Produce £100,000 of unit trust money in a month.
- Do five mortgage related cases.
- Produce £50,000 of new annualised premium income (select your own time scale).
- Write a £1,000,000 of life cover in four weeks.
- Write a £1,000,000 policy on one person.
- Produce an executive retirement plan every week for eight weeks.

Mini goals such as these bring with them their own sense of urgency because they have the additional feature all goals must have

— a deadline. A goal without a deadline can never be exciting because there is no purpose to it. It would be like a race with no finishing line. You would just never know when, or even if, you had won.

Man always works better when he has a goal. The reasons for his goal may differ. Anger, pride, glory, ego, need, frustration or as the mountaineers would say, "Just because they are there." It doesn't matter why, but if you want to achieve you have to set them.

CHAPTER 10

Golden Rules

SIX THOUSAND life insurance salespeople from 44 countries sat in a darkened giant auditorium in Hawaii waiting for the Million Dollar Round Table Annual Meeting to begin. I looked around and spent a few moments wondering what characteristics they had in common. It was obvious they came in all shapes and sizes, male and female and with a variety of skin colours, yet they shared one thing in common. They had all qualified to attend the MDRT Annual Meeting.

Since then I have made it my practice to study the habits of successful agents in order to try to identify what they do differently that sets them apart from the average agent. Perhaps not to my surprise, whilst successful agents individually have their own personal traits and characteristics, in contrast as a group they share most, if not all, of the Golden Rules I have accumulated over my years of observation.

GOLDEN RULE NO.1

PERPETUALLY PROSPECT. "Set aside an hour a day for prospecting" is advice you will read in many books on selling. It is wrong. By implication the rest of the day you do not need to prospect and as a result you don't!

Prospecting is something you should be doing continually every minute of the day. Think about your average day. How many people do you come into contact with in your ordinary daily life? Very conservatively I would suggest a minimum of 10, and more likely nearer 20. Without exception everyone of them will have a need for one of our products, if not today then at sometime in the future. What is more they are part of their own 'nest' and if nothing else could give you at least two introductions.

During my years in management the most overworked excuse for lack of production has always been, "My problem is I do not have any prospects." I recall being in the London office of an outstanding manager when one of his agents came in and said the same thing. My host took the agent to the window, pulled back the blind, pointed down to the thousands of people scurrying along Oxford Street and said, "How could you be short of prospects when there are all those people right outside our door, most of whom have totally inadequate life assurance, pension and investment arrangements?"

Prospecting should be like shaving in the morning or, if you are a lady agent, putting on your make-up! A routine habit which you do without thinking. Very few people are natural born prospectors. You simply have to make it a habit which you do not have to think about but which becomes part of your ordinary daily life.

You need to learn the art of listening to what people say rather than merely hearing their words. For example, in casual conversation with your newsagent, he might say, "I'm not my usual self this morning because we were out very late at my father's retirement party." The average reply would be, "I know how you feel." The listening life insurance agent would go on to say, "Tell me, has your father been a member of a pension scheme, and if so do you know what he plans to do with his lump sum?"

Another example. You get talking to a businessman at a party and he tells you he has a very busy week because his company is expanding and they are negotiating for some new premises. "I am glad to hear things are going well", you might say, but if you are really switched on you'll then ask him, "May I ask how you propose to finance the purchase?"

Most true prospecting opportunities arise automatically during ordinary conversation. If you have developed the philosophy of perpetual prospecting and not restricted yourself to one hour a day, you should never need to join the ranks of the agents who complain they do not have any prospects.

GOLDEN RULE NO.2

PLAN TOMORROW TODAY. Have you ever suffered the embarrassment of sitting in front of a prospect who decides to buy, only to discover you have no trust form with you? Even an application? Of course you have; it has happened to all of us!

How often are you late for an appointment and rush in, flustered, blaming the traffic conditions when in reality you just did not leave your office early enough. This sort of think puts you at a disadvantage and is not conducive to good interviews.

One of the reasons the truly successful agents can be so busy, and yet always appear to have time on their side is because they plan tomorrow today. It isn't because they are particularly clever or by nature disciplined and organised. Invariably they have learned the hard way, having made the mistake of leaving everything to the last minute only to find the most important items get overlooked.

My 'next week's planning' starts on Saturday morning when I review my appointments schedule. If there are illustrations to prepare in advance of meetings I get them done. I make sure I place within each file all the forms and paperwork I am likely to need. However well run your office, from time to time supplies run out and it is very frustrating to discover, just as you dash out of the office, that the very form you want is out of stock!

I file Tuesday to Friday's appointments in my pending drawer, sort Monday's into 'running' order and leave them on my desk. All I have to do is grab the file and run! I know it is complete. Similar planning is required for every formal meeting you arrange. The boardroom is prepared the night before with flip chart, overhead projector, note pads, copies of presentation, and whatever else is going to be required. You do not go home at night until tomorrow is totally ready.

I compile a list of all the phone calls I need to make with their numbers, sort the files into running order and then plan the time when the phone call will be made.

Planning tomorrow today is one of the most successful strategies of good time management. The people who panic are those who do not plan and prepare.

GOLDEN RULE NO.3

ALWAYS BE CONFIDENT. I was due to speak on the main platform at the Wembley Conference Centre many years ago. This is not the easiest of settings because the auditorium is circular and the audience sit all around the stage. A few weeks before, I had the opportunity to watch a master speaker on the same platform and he was kind enough to give freely of his time and his advice to me about my forthcoming presentation. One phrase he used remains in my mind to this day. "Ken, just remember, when you go on that stage, act as if. Act as if you have done it many times before. Only you know it's the first time; your audience doesn't. Do not disillusion them!"

He was absolutely right. "Whenever I feel afraid I whistle a happy tune", sang Anna in *'The King and I'*. That is the same thing but, of course, you would cause some consternation if you went into a major appointment and, to hide your nervousness, started whistling! Far better to 'act as if' because you will not only appear confident, before long you will actually become confident.

Naturally, 'planning tomorrow today' helps because at least you know there can be no unpleasant surprises. However, there is something else you need to do.

Knowledge really is power; if you have done your homework you have little or nothing to fear, because from knowledge comes not only power but confidence and authority. There is an added advantage. Your prospect or client will have confidence in you if you have confidence in yourself. Should you appear apprehensive or uncertain, your listener will feel uneasy and is less likely to take your advice.

GOLDEN RULE NO.4

FIND MARKETS WHERE YOU FEEL COMFORTABLE. "Stick to your knitting" and "Cobbler stick to your last" are other phrases which could be used to describe this Golden Rule.

Clearly, it is closely related to Golden Rule No.3. If you deliberately place yourself in markets where you are uncomfortable you will certainly not appear confident. The trouble is, the grass on the other side of the fence always appears greener, but you know it's usually harder to mow! Why bother about it when your own grass has a habit of growing two or three inches every week! Having said that, there is no reason why you should not plan to move into other markets but you need to find out something about them first of all.

When I first decided to try my hand at prospecting seminars I went to other people's to find out what was going on. I did not restrict myself to the insurance industry either; if there was a seminar on any subject within 20 miles I was interested because I wanted to find out what other people were doing.

I will not say I had become aware of all the potential problems before I stood on the platform for my own first seminar, but I was certainly able to avoid many of the mistakes I saw others make. As a result I was comfortable and confident from the beginning and made the transition from individual to group prospecting with no real difficulties.

GOLDEN RULE NO.5

DON'T KEEP TRYING TO RE-INVENT THE WHEEL. I am not against progress but we should never stray far from the good old fashioned tried and tested basic ideas which have worked in the past, and will work in the future.

Talking to a group of salesmen some years ago, Lyle Blessman, a prolific producer from Colorado said he was still doing today exactly what he was doing 26 years ago. Somebody asked him why, and his reply was illuminating: "Because I find it keeps on working — and working — and working, so why should I change?" Certainly we need to work smarter, but in my book that means making a better job of doing what we have always been doing anyway. I knew one agent who had to drop everything he had been doing and focus on each new idea the moment he came across it. A new product would be launched and for the next six months it would command his total attention. Time and again he would finally wake up to discover his production had fallen away almost to zero, yet he never learned his lesson.

Once you find out what works for you, just go on doing it. If you come across something new see it as an addition and not a substitution for what you have been doing. For example, most agents start off focusing on domestic business, but before long the attractions of the corporate market begin to appeal. The wise agent would allocate only one day a week to the development of this new market, taking the work from that day and adding a quarter of it to the remaining four days of the week. As he begins to become successful with business assurance he will make a further change, perhaps spending two days on it until he feels the correct ratios have been established.

GOLDEN RULE NO.6

NEVER STOP LEARNING. "We live in an age of change" is certainly a well known phrase or saying. Every age has been one of change, but, of course, the difference now is the pace. Things happen much faster now than they used to and we have to keep up to date. There is certainly no shortage of material nowadays to help us! Indeed, the danger is that there is a surfeit of it and, as a result, important changes get overlooked.

Studying is down time activity and needs to have specific hours allocated to it. Ben Feldman tells the story of his early days in the business when he made it a practice to spend one hour every day reading the rate book. Quite often he did not understand everything he was reading, but nevertheless he persevered. It would not surprise me to find that Ben to this day is doing the same thing.

I take just about every insurance magazine and paper published. I am also on the mailing list for a specialist tax publication which produces fortnightly bulletins.

I have made it a habit to attend at least two conferences outside our industry each year. One is the Institute of Directors Annual Convention, and the second will be a tax-related conference. I am looking for ideas that help not only me but my clients, because what I learn could be of use to them.

I do not believe you can stay up to date in the 90s unless you are prepared to devote at least two hours every week to doing so.

GOLDEN RULE NO.7

INVEST IN YOUR BUSINESS. A survey of the MDRT members recently indicated they invest, on average, some 40 per cent of their gross income back into their business for one purpose or another — and this is in addition to the amount they might spend on staff salaries and the like.

A significant amount is spent on office equipment and, in particular, computers and word processors. If you want to produce top quality work you need the best back-up equipment. You probably need a computerised client and prospect data base, spread sheet programmes and, for the more sophisticated, monthly updated investment statistics, all on your computer.

I am 'writing' these words using a dictating machine, which naturally requires playback equipment. A telephone in the car and the mobile in the briefcase I now regard as essential rather than luxury items, and I would not travel far without my programmable pocket calculator.

The business conferences I attend each year, I regard certainly as an investment back into my business. Over and above that, however, there are the annual insurance conventions which should be 'a must'. It has been a constant mystery to me why so many people in our industry fail to attend the Life Insurance Association's Annual Convention at London's Barbican Centre or, for those who qualify, the MDRT Annual Meeting in the United States.

The first time I spoke at MDRT myself in Hawaii the legendary Ben Feldman sat in the front row. I thanked him afterwards for coming along to hear my talk, from which I assumed he could have learned nothing, because almost everything I said had originally come from people like himself. He explained that he had written 12 million dollars of business during my talk because things I said reminded him of people who needed our product. When the likes of Ben Feldman stop going to conventions, so will I, but in the meantime I regard them as an essential part of my annual business expenditure.

GOLDEN RULE NO.8

DREAM. If you want to achieve big things you first have to dream big dreams, said Conrad Hilton, founder of the international hotel organisation. Everyone needs to have a number of dreams to act as their own personal motivator. I used to wonder who motivated the motivator but now I know — he motivates himself, and he does it by having dreams, goals and ambitions.

One thing is certain: your achievements will rarely exceed your dreams, so dream big.

GOLDEN RULE NO.9

HAVE SUFFICIENT INTERVIEWS. This one seems so basic and yet most people who fail in our industry or never hit the heights of real success do so because they fail to see enough people.

Studying the statistics of top producers I have observed that their average case size is not as large as you would expect. There may only be a 10 per cent difference between the cases produced by the average agent and those right at the pinnacle of our profession. The difference, quite clearly, is in the number of cases produced; that is directly related to the number of meetings held.

I believe the goal should be 16 meetings a week. After all, that is only four a day with one day allocated for office work.

One top producer I know holds his meetings at 10 am, 12 noon, 2 pm and 4 pm. He will not hold them at any other time because if he varied he would not get in four a day. He is only allowed to make client appointments for morning meetings; his secretary is allocated the afternoon. It is a very simple and extremely effective system which enables him to produce at Top of the Table level every year.

The average agent tries to succeed on maybe six meetings a week and then wonders why he is constantly struggling. You lift the pressure off yourself and your prospects if you have enough of them. I know you occasionally hear of a 'mega producer' who claims only to have three or four meetings a week. There is always an exception to the rule, but most of us are ordinary mortals who are incapable of that kind of performance.

GOLDEN RULE NO.10

DELEGATE TO OTHERS WHENEVER POSSIBLE. Back to time planning, of course, but first you must have someone to whom you can delegate. The most successful agents are extraordinarily good at this. I call it the 'dump and run' principle, and employ the 3 Ds — Delegate it, Ditch it or Do it.

I judge my own personal success on a daily basis by how little I have left to do from the paperwork which has come in the mail, how much is in the waste paper basket, and the amount I have been able to delegate to somebody else.

GOLDEN RULE NO.11

KNOW YOUR STRENGTHS AND WEAKNESSES. Most of us go through life utilising a large part of our energies in trying to improve the things at which we are weak. I came to the conclusion a few years ago that after a lifetime of trying (and failing), I was unlikely to change any of the things at which I was weak and that I ought to use my efforts in a more positive direction. After much soul searching I decided the one particular strength I had was my confidence and enjoyment of being on my feet in front of a group of people. This led directly to the use of seminars and I have simply worked to make each one better than the last.

My weaknesses? As the staff around me will tell you, I delegate to them. Strangely enough, they are strong where I am not. If you are not able to be honest with yourself in carrying out this analysis, by the way, ask someone else — but be prepared for some shocks.

GOLDEN RULE NO.12

ALWAYS BE PREPARED TO SERVICE WHAT YOU SELL. If what you have sold is right, you will always take pleasure in servicing it. If you ever need to cross the road to avoid talking to a client, then you are not abiding by this Golden Rule, and are skating on thin ice. You know servicing makes sense, but it's being proud to do so which adds an extra dimension to your entire philosophy of life.

GOLDEN RULE NO.13

STUDY THE WORK HABITS OF SUCCESSFUL PEOPLE. Most successful people got there either by making many mistakes themselves and learning their lessons, or by learning from the mistakes made by other people.

It seems obvious to me that the agent leading the branch or his company is not only doing a lot of things right, but very few wrong. If you can only find out how he works it will increase your own chances of becoming truly successful.

The nice thing is, most successful people are only too willing to share their 'secrets' with those less fortunate. I have lost count of the number of times I have been privileged to sit down with one of the industry legends, and for him to spend an hour or more telling me the way he works and of the mistakes he has made which I should avoid. We have an enviable reputation for sharing in this industry; you only have to ask and, my word, you do receive.

In any event, people like being asked, don't they? It's the greatest compliment you can pay someone. The man who is confident in his own ability does not fear that by sharing his secrets he will increase the pressure of competition.

If you wanted to improve your tennis, would you want to play with the club rabbit or the champion? You would pick the champion every time because you would hope to learn from the way he plays. It is just the same in our business.

GOLDEN RULE NO.14

BE THE BEST LIFE AGENT IN TOWN. It takes a lifetime to earn a good reputation and you can lose it with one bad act.

You must have an on-going commitment to be the best you can be. Dedicate yourself to the highest standards of professional and ethical behaviour. Earn the reputation of always being willing to go the extra mile on behalf of your clients. Always put your clients' interests first, and your own a very poor second.

★ ★ ★ ★ ★

I try to run my business on the basis of these Golden Rules. Now it is a ritual; each came from my own personal study of the work habits of successful people. There are very few solid guarantees nowadays, but there is no doubt at all that if you follow the Golden Rules you too will become more successful than you are today, no matter at what level you are performing.

CHAPTER 11

Clark's Laws

WHILST I TRULY ADMIT none of the Golden Rules in the preceding chapter is original, I can say that, as far as I know, all of Clark's Laws are.

If the title sounds a little arrogant, forgive me. They are laws I have devised to help me to stay 'on track'. Who knows, some of them may help you as well. Most of them are the outcome of a particular set of circumstances in which I found myself when I had to rationalise my situation or, in some cases, motivate myself to go on. All in all, combined with the Golden Rules, they provide the basic philosophy for my business practice although, I must confess, there are times when I have to be reminded of them.

YOU SELL A LAPSE AT THE POINT OF SALE

Our product is probably unique. With most goods and services a salesman completes a deal and that's the end of it. His customer will pay cash and the deal is done. If he is buying an item on hire purchase, the salesman does his job and then it is up to the hire purchase company to collect the money for payments.

In our industry it is a little different. With the power of your oratory, the force of your presence or by being a persistent nuisance, you might persuade your prospect to purchase one of your products. He retains the whip hand however; the moment you have gone out of the door and 'buyer's remorse' sets in (or he realises he has purchased something he does not really want) he can drop a note to his bank, cancel the direct debit, and the sale does not go through.

Furthermore, he retains that power throughout the lifetime of the policy. If at any time he feels what you have sold him isn't right, he can stop payments. This is most likely to happen when another agent moves in and creates doubt in your client's mind. If he has not truly 'bought' your solution in the fullest sense of the word, his confidence may be shaken and you suddenly have a lapse on your hands.

A well sold case — or to put it more accurately, a well bought case — will not lapse. No one will be able to move in behind you and cause your client to doubt his actions.

The best way to ensure this is by sticking to the Broad Concept principle. It results in people buying, rather than you selling. You still need to consolidate and the best way to do this is to use the policy summary sheet I recommended in Chapter 5 and on which you show the reason why your policy was purchased. If, for example, you have written something like, "To ensure my wife Karen and my children Justin and Louise have sufficient income in the event of my death", your client is very unlikely to be persuaded by an unscrupulous agent that the policy should be terminated.

A PROSPECT IS A CLIENT WHO HAS NOT YET BOUGHT FROM YOU

It is extremely rare if not impossible to find a prospect who has purchased his last life assurance, pensions or investment policy. Consequently, almost everybody you talk to is a potential client either for now or in the future. The way you conduct yourself with that person could determine whether or not you are the agent from whom he buys his next policy. Treat him right when there is no prospect of immediate business and you enhance the likelihood of getting the next case.

Bear in mind, also, you are looking not just for immediate business, but for recommendations. If you show displeasure because your prospect declines to do business with you at the present time, you close the door for ever. Turn it to your advantage. Properly handled your prospect will feel a degree of moral responsibility if he should decide not to buy from you, and in a strange way it makes it easier to get recommendations.

Some years ago I chose to buy my car from a local garage because they gave me a particularly good deal. Shortly thereafter their depot was closed and servicing of my vehicle was taken over by a supplier whose offer I had originally declined. Over the next five years that garage gave me superb service. They could not have done better had I bought the original vehicle from them.

Needless to say, when the time came to change, this time I did not even shop around. I was not worried whether I could have got a better deal elsewhere. The garage had earned the right to my business because it had treated me like a client even though for five years I was simply a prospect. It got the business and will get the next deal I do too.

JUDGE YOURSELF BY WHAT YOU HAVE ACHIEVED — NOT BY WHAT YOU HAVE LEFT UNDONE

Despite being the author of the law I have to remind myself about it quite frequently!

It all starts by attempting too much, and an inability to say no, to which I made reference in the chapter on Time Management. At the end of an incredibly busy day you look at your desk — and the pile of work needing your attention seems to have grown even larger. It can be very depressing and demoralising.

After one particularly bad day which left me feeling tense and extremely irritated, I spent some time reviewing what I had actually achieved during the day. I asked myself, could I have done more? I came to the conclusion it had been a remarkably successful day based upon what I had actually done. Twelve hours virtually non-stop and I had moved a veritable mountain of work. The fact that I still had a tremendous amount left to do was actually irrelevant because there was no way I could have got through any more than I did. Immediately my spirits lifted and the third of Clark's Laws came into being.

It is inevitable that as you become more busy the work load will increase; there will be days when you finish with more on your desk than you started. When that happens sit quietly for a few moments and evaluate what you have actually achieved. That should be your standard of judgement. The rest of the work just gets carried forward to the next day.

WHERE YOU ARE TODAY IS DETERMINED BY WHERE YOU WANT TO BE TOMORROW

This is somewhat subtle. Many people think that where you are today determines where you will be tomorrow, and in a way it does, but that is a little negative. It seems to carry with it the suggestion that you cannot control your destiny.

As people who always try to retain a positive outlook on life, we need to feel at all times that we are in control and master of our own destiny. I believe it is something to do with critical path analysis. This is the somewhat simplistic way in which I see it:

Some years ago a decision was taken to build a bridge over the River Orwell which runs through Ipswich down to the sea at Felixstowe. The objective was to enable people to get from one side of the river to the other without going through town centre, and clearly to make the journey quicker, if not shorter. In planning the construction of the bridge, the engineers decided to start from either bank, meeting in the middle.

Now it would have been no good at all for team 'A' and team 'B' to start their work in the fond hope that ultimately they would by some miracle meet exactly where they wanted to in the middle of the river. They did it the other way around. They calculated where they wanted to meet and then worked backwards step by step in their planning until each team got back to its respective bank. Then, and only then, were they able to plan their strategy. They knew where they wanted to be tomorrow and this determined where they had to start today.

In planning our enterprise, we should say, "Where do I want to be five years from now?" Having determined that, we then step back one month, one year, at a time until ultimately we discover what we should be doing today.

For example, let us assume your objective is to create a turnover of quarter of a million pounds five years from now, with two selling assistants generating at least a third of the total business. What should your production be four years from now; three years, two, one? In order to be certain that your selling assistants are producing at the level you require five years from now, what will their build-up of business be? What amount of training would you give them? How long would this take and, therefore, when should you actually put them under contract?

Deciding where you are today pre-determines where you will be tomorrow, and to that extent it will be out of your control. Take control by setting your goals first; then step backwards until you arrive at today.

DOUBLE FACE TO FACE TIME AND YOU WILL DOUBLE YOUR BUSINESS

I believe this law actually understates the true position. If you are successful in doubling the face to face time you have with clients and prospects, I actually believe you will more than double your business. You will become increasingly proficient, a better prospector and your closing ratio will improve.

Do you want to double your business? Most people do, but it looks a daunting prospect. Remember, however, you are only likely to be spending 16 per cent of your time face to face with prospects or clients. By judicious management of your time you should be able to get this up to 30 per cent or more without too much difficulty. Even so, doubling whatever is your current production in a 12 month period probably looks impossible, so let me show you a different way of viewing it.

Last year it took you 12 months to produce your full year's quota of business. Effectively, there were people you finally managed to turn into clients in December, who had actually been there all year; for one reason or another you did not get to them until December. The need, for most of them, had existed for 12 months and you simply made them wait.

What you need to do is to shorten the timescale. Do not set out to double your business in 12 months; plan to write the same amount of business in half the time. You are now dealing with a time management problem which is relatively easy to solve. When 30th June comes along and you have just about equalled last year's production, all you have to do is to repeat the exercise over the next six months. Wonder of wonders, by 31st December you have doubled your production.

THE TRUE MEASURE OF SUCCESS IS BEATING YOUR PERSONAL BEST

I get extremely irritated when I listen to commentators at athletic events only lauding the person who came first and "Won the Gold Medal". This to me is not necessarily the best achievement in the race. I see little to enthuse about if the person who won did not actually achieve his or her own personal best. In reality they under-performed, and I do not really see that to be justification for undue celebration.

l be the person who came last had the most outstanding f all, beating his own personal best by the greatest

loves a winner, it is said, but it is the standard of measurement we use which is extremely important. Only one person can go past the finishing line first. In that respect we would have to call him a winner. It does not mean, however, that second, third and fourth — and even last — should be regarded as losers. In the terms of personal achievement they may well have produced their finest performance ever; that surely is how they should be judged.

In our goal setting, therefore, this is the standard of measurement we should use for ourselves. To be continually motivated we should always see ourselves as winners, and the standards we apply should be ours and not someone else's.

Let me give you a new personal competition you might like to try. Set out to have your best 12 individual months ever. Look back over your records and select your best January, your best February, your best March and so on. Add them all together, increase by say 20 per cent, and that is your target for the next 12 months. At the end of the year you may well be number 1,000 in your company, but it doesn't matter; if you have had your best 12 months ever, then you will know the meaning of true success.

A MAN EARNS THE RIGHT TO INVEST OR MAKE PENSION PROVISION BY BUYING ADEQUATE PROTECTION IN THE FORM OF LIFE INSURANCE AND DISABILITY COVER

That is my longest rule and rightly so, because it is so fundamentally important. Ben Feldman says: "The contracts I sell are for time and money. If you don't have the time I produce the money. If you have too much time, I produce the money."

That is the fundamental business we are in. It is why we sell assurance and our non-life colleagues sell insurance. They insure payments will be made in respect of events that *might* happen. We on the other hand assure payments will be made in respect of events which *will* happen. Death, retirement and disability come under those headings.

My very firmly held belief for many years has been that an individual must first put his house in order by arranging adequate protection for his family or his business in the form of life assurance and disability cover. He can plan for his retirement and investment needs with some degree of certainty. There is no certainty on how long he will remain alive, fit and well. He should not, therefore, consider any form of investment until he has made adequate provision for what I like to call the catastrophe risk.

One of my colleagues puts it this way. Life assurance and protection recommendations are mandatory and non-negotiable. Anything else is desirable and optional, but he will not move to stage 2 — and will not even have the prospect as a client — unless he accepts the stage 1 recommendations.

THE DOMESTIC MARKET TENDS TO BE COST DRIVEN — THE CORPORATE MARKET IS MORE LIKELY TO BE NEEDS DRIVEN

The point about this law is that the domestic market ebbs and flows according to the time of year and the demands upon the public's purses! Holidays, Christmas, Easter, weddings, christenings, birthdays, funerals — all can be used as justifiable reasons why this is not the right time to discuss life assurance. People have a limited budget and their own sense of priorities.

The corporate business is more likely to be a 12 month market. The need for pension planning, commercial loans, keyman and share protection and partnership cover are always there. A business is likely to have a greater control over its cash flow than a private individual. Furthermore, corporate cheques tend to be bigger than those drawn on a personal account, which enables the focus to be on the need rather than the cost.

IF YOU DON'T SERVE THEM YOU DON'T DESERVE THEM

When you buy a share in a public company you are actually buying the right to a stream of future income. Provided you continue to hold the share and the company trades successfully, that income in the form of dividends is guaranteed.

When you acquire a new client you do not automatically earn the right to a stream of future income in the form of renewal commission, increases or recommendations. They will not come automatically.

Whenever I go to the Annual Meeting of Million Dollar Round Table, I remind myself of the debt I owe to my clients. They got me there, but I like to think it is not all one way. With more than 70 per cent of my new production each year coming from existing clients, I have to take some credit for the standard of service I provide.

If you are getting less than 40 per cent of your production from existing clients, if your lapse rate is more than 10 per cent, the chances are you are not providing the level of service you should be, and you do not deserve the loyalty of your clients.

BYE-LAWS

There are a vast number of Clark's Bye-Laws but those are truly personal to the way I work. No doubt you have your own.

I do find that whenever I ignore any of them, I do so at my peril. It always costs me and I resolve never to forget them again. It is rather like the speed limit. You know the law, but from time to time you ignore it. Most times you get away with it but every now and again you get caught. You may well succeed most of the time without your own set of rules, but the need for them is there. If you don't know them you certainly will one day and get caught out — and it can be an expensive and costly surprise.

CHAPTER 12

Turning Points

"*WHAT DO YOU KNOW ABOUT MDRT?*"

Life is sprinkled with events which seem insignificant at the time but, on reflection, weeks, months, even years later are seen to have had a major effect on destiny. These singular items become turning points in a lifetime or a career. Little was I to know, when Jerry Pore of Metropolitan Life in Fort Walton Beach, Florida, addressed that simple question to me, the effect upon my business career would be so dramatic.

As I sat in his office that Wednesday afternoon on 24th June 1970 he told me about the Million Dollar Round Table. In fact he had just returned from the Annual Meeting in Hawaii, and was full of enthusiasm about the speakers and presentations it had been his privilege to hear.

My sole purpose in meeting with Jerry was the hope that the costs of a holiday could be offset in part, if not in whole, against my tax, by having what I claimed to be a business meeting with an insurance agent. As Jerry explained to me the whole man concept and the philosophy of Million Dollar Round Table, I realised this was truly something big — and was without doubt a business meeting.

That two hour meeting prompted me to make a major decision as I flew back across the Atlantic two days later. I would sell off the non-life side of my brokerage to focus on life assurance. My second decision was to qualify for MDRT the following year.

Jerry introduced me to Metropolitan's London agent, Woody Woodall, and through him I met Clive Holmes. In time that led to the formation of the Life Insurance Association. Woody lent me a number of audio cassettes of live recordings made at previous MDRT meetings and I began to listen to people who, amazingly, seemed to tell a very similar story to myself — up to a point. The majority appeared to have been performing in their business lives at a modest level until some event occurred which became a turning point for them. Maybe the same thing was happening to me.

Those cassettes gave me the motivation I needed to see me through 1971, but it was not until December I finally issued the last case I needed to qualify for MDRT. Six months later, on 26th June 1972, I sat in the Place Des Arts in Montreal, Canada, and heard the 45th President, James B. Longley, open the Annual Meeting with the following words:

> "This is the beginning of a new week.
> You have been given this week to use as you will.
> You can waste it or use it for good.
> What you do this week is important because you are exchanging a week of your lives for it.
> When next week comes this week will be gone forever,
> leaving in its place something that you have traded for it.
> May it be gain, not loss, good not evil, success not failure,
> in order that you shall never regret the price you have paid for it — a week in your lives.
> Peace."

It was indeed not just the beginning of a new week, but the start of a totally new attitude, and it is that which has directed my business career every since.

There were some quite outstanding presentations that week in Montreal. Much of the credit for the chapter in this book on Time Planning must go to Bill O'Donnell who spoke on the subject. I made pages of notes which I have to this day.

I learned about factfinding and returned to the United Kingdom enthusiastic and with a 32 page version I intended to use at once. I must confess I soon reduced it to 16 pages and even then hardly used it. An A4 pad (now supplemented by a portable dictating machine) has served me very well, but the point is, I learned the principle.

The last morning was an experience I shall re-live over and over again in my mind, when Rulon Rasmussen closed the meeting with his incredible presentation 'Does Anybody Care'. Be sure I certainly cared after I heard it, and as a result of that memorable occasion I have since attended more than a dozen such Annual Meetings in some amazing locations in various parts of the United States. Without exception every meeting has given me a host of new ideas and has in itself been a further turning point.

For instance, it was at MDRT that I first heard someone talk about Breakfast Clubs — so I started one. Where do you think I learned about seminars? MDRT. The value of record keeping? Goal setting, the psychology of the sale? The list is endless, and the credit all goes to the Million Dollar Round Table.

The role of the salespeople in our industry is not easy. You have to take plenty of knocks and learn to bounce back. We hear much about rejection but personally I do not find that a great problem. It is frustration which gets to me when I realise how much people need our product and yet how little aware they are of it themselves. With the average in-force life insurance policy only providing around £14,000 of cover, we need never fear our market will become saturated!

CONTINUAL MOTIVATION

I must now have around 350 audio cassettes of MDRT speeches, together with the Proceedings Manuals, going back to 1969. They are a veritable gold mine of every conceivable sales idea and business management concept you could possible imagine. However, they contain something else which I find even more valuable — that is the power to motivate, or as one of the speakers in Montreal put it — to undemotivate.

From time to time we all find ourselves 'down'. Maybe it is rejection or frustration, the loss of a big case or the death of one of our clients. When that happens you need a 'pick me up'. What I do is simply make a selection from my library of tapes or articles. It is the finest medicine I can take. I defy anybody to stay depressed after listening to some of the greats from within and outside our industry who have walked the boards of MDRT.

Attending the Annual Meeting gives my batteries a full charge. My tape library and the Proceedings Manuals provide a booster throughout the year. I could not survive without them.

The next best thing, of course, is to get involved with the Life Insurance Association and attend its Annual Convention at the Barbican, which is really a mini MDRT. Also there is the opportunity to attend monthly meetings held throughout the country where salespeople share freely their very best sales ideas. I do not know another industry where that happens.

A MAGNIFICENT OBSESSION

I was very fortunate. For the first 23 years after I left school I had a job in the insurance industry. I looked upon it as a not unpleasant way of earning a living, and worked reasonably hard at it. I expected to go on doing the same thing until I earned an honourable retirement at 65!

Then came the turning points. The first was learning about the Million Dollar Round Table. The second was attending my first MDRT meeting and the third was involvement with others on a dream which finally became the Life Insurance Association. Each convention, every meeting since then has brought with it a turning point; some merely a minor change of direction, others a major new initiative. No one has a monopoly on good ideas and I like to be amongst people who are willing to share what they have.

As I perched on my stool in the office of the Alliance Assurance Company in 1949, I never imagined that one day I would be standing on a platform addressing a meeting of some of the world's top insurance salespeople. Million Dollar Round Table made that happen for me. It could do the same for you.

CHAPTER 13

My One Hundred and One Best Ideas

EVERY CORDON BLEU Chef worth his salt compiles his own special recipe book. The top comedians constantly update their joke books. Accountants have a library of reference books and solicitors' offices are lined floor to ceiling with Law Reports. These books are the stock in trade of the professionals. When they need a solution to a problem, feel the need for inspiration or just simply want to try something different they know where to look.

The stock in trade of a life insurance agent consists of ideas. At the first time orientation session of the Montreal MDRT meeting, my table host was a French Canadian, Benny Chartier. He gave us many pearls of wisdom that day; one of the best was his advice never to go to a meeting without a pad and pen. "Build up a sales idea book", he said, "it will be your saviour over and over again in the years ahead."

I did just that and now have two filing cabinet drawers absolutely crammed with notes I have made from the hundreds of meetings I have attended.

Time and again I have fallen back on them when I found myself to be in a slump, when preparing a speech or writing an article. I have gathered together in the following pages what I consider to be the 101 best ideas to form a 'self-contained reference book' which you can dip into whenever you have the need.

I have loosely divided them into prospecting and sales ideas, together with half a dozen 'miscellaneous'. In fact, prospecting and sales ideas overlap. For example, if you meet someone at a party, and after finding out what business you are in, he asks if you are busy, you might reply, "As a matter of fact I am absolutely rushed off my feet. People seem to have suddenly realised how important it is to cover their mortgage payments with disability insurance." That is both a subtle prospecting approach and a sales idea; indeed it might even be a close as well.

Mainly Prospecting

It is generally agreed the best way of prospecting is through introductions and recommendations. However, there seems to be a natural reluctance to 'ask the question' but there is more than one way to skin a rabbit!

My first few ideas focus on this area.

1. A POWERFUL QUESTION

"John, Mary, if you had both been killed in a car accident yesterday, who would be getting your children ready for school in future?"

This is a perfect example of an approach which can produce introductions as well as substantial business in the domestic sector.

Very few parents with young children have considered the position in which their relatives and friends could find themselves in the event of their untimely death. It is clearly a most stressful situation to imagine, but that is no excuse for not facing up to reality.

I first asked the question of a farmer and his wife who had three young children. At my insistence they finally telephoned their choice of guardian — the wife's sister and her husband — who agreed to the appointment. Having secured the introduction I was seeking I also was able to persuade my prospects to 'fund' the guardianship by effecting substantial life assurance, something they had refused to consider until my somewhat dramatic question.

It does amuse me that couples will often travel on separate airplanes and yet drive to the airport in the same car! Clearly, the problem is at the back of their minds, but it needs someone like us to bring it to the fore.

2. GRANDPARENTS

Grandparents are always fond of their grandchildren! Suggest they set up a special trust fund for them, using a savings plan. It could help pay school fees, buy their first car or pay for a wedding.

There is another angle. Grandparents may have a vested interest in their sons' and daughters' life assurance programme. After all, they could suddenly find themselves with young children to bring up if tragedy struck the parents!

3. WHO ARE YOUR EXECUTORS?

Everybody has a Will, either one they have made themselves or the one the Government has made for them under the Intestacy Act.

If they have made a Will almost certainly it includes the appointment of Executors. After arranging some life assurance it is surely appropriate for you to meet the Executors to explain what you are doing. After all, it may well fall upon them to administer some of the funds you are helping your clients to create. Another quality introduction, and no need to use the word 'referral' or even to ask for help!

Should there not yet be a personal Will, you simply enquire who the Executors will be when it is written, and proceed to step 2.

4. I AM YOUR EXECUTOR

Invite your prospect to imagine the following scene. Sadly, he died yesterday and you are his Executor. In five minutes' time his widow is coming in to see you. "John, what do you think is the question which will be uppermost in her mind?" Undoubtedly, what is her financial situation.

"What can I tell her? Can I reassure her that she has no worries because you have provided for her future with adequate life assurance or do I have to gently break the news that she will have to survive on not much more than a widow's pension? John, you are the only one who can decide what my answer will be."

5. PUT YOUR TRUST IN A TRUST

In the vast majority of cases, all life assurance benefits should be written in trust. Trustees will be required, especially if there are young children involved, and indeed, some companies make it relatively easy for you, because trustees are required to sign the form of appointment.

Whether or not that is the case, it is the responsibility of the agent to visit the trustees and explain what will be their duties under the trust. Would it not be natural whilst you are there to say, "Could I take the opportunity to talk to you about your life assurance, pension and investment programme?"

6. THE ROLE OF THE GODPARENT

Ask your prospects if they are godparents to any young children.

When my niece was born I became her godfather and realised that when she was 18 I would want to give her a really nice present. As you might expect, I took out an endowment policy for her and I am very proud of the photograph I have of Jane sitting on the Hunter she bought with the proceeds of that gift.

Now let us look at it the other way. Do your clients have children and, if so, are there godparents? I feel certain they would be more than willing to give you an introduction so that you can talk about this little idea.

7. A QUICKIE

"Who are the two most successful men you know?" A simple question guaranteed to produce two high quality prospects.

8. PLANT A PROSPECTING TREE

Most people are familiar with the family tree. Why not plant a prospecting tree? Explain to your client or prospect that you plan to build a new form of family tree. His name is at the top and below it on the first two branches will be the names of the two introductions he has given you. When you visit each of them you finish up by asking exactly the same question, getting two more introductions. (Of course, one may be the person who sent you there in the first instance; when that happens you simply ask for another one.)

You add the four new names onto the spreading branches of your tree and off you go again.

Whenever any of the introductions become a client you highlight their name on your tree. This, of course, will intrigue the people to whom you show it and they are bound to ask what the highlights mean. Without giving away any details, you simply explain those are the people who have already become clients of yours.

From time to time go back up the tree showing everybody what has happened. I guarantee they will be very interested and pleased at the way they have been able to help you. They will also be fascinated to find people in the prospecting tree they have never actually met themselves, and you might now begin to arrange some introductions which could perhaps lead to additional business for everybody concerned.

9. PROFILE OF A PROSPECT

Ideally you should have a clear picture in your mind of the sort of person you want as a client. It would help your introducer if you prepare a profile and show it to him.

Do you know this man?

1. He is aged between 25 and 50.
2. His income is between £10,000 and £25,000 a year.
3. He earns his living:
   (a) Running his own business.
   (b) As a professional man.
   (c) As a senior executive in a large company.
4. He is married.
5. He almost certainly has a mortgage.
6. There is a young family.

You can draw up a number of profiles to show to a variety of prospects.

10. ASKING FOR INTRODUCTIONS IN ADVANCE

"John, as you know I met you as a result of an introduction from our mutual friend. What I am going to do now is take you through one of our standard financial planning questionnaires and when we come to the end, whether or not we do any business together, I am going to put a question to you. I am going to ask whether you have been entirely happy with the way I have conducted our meeting. If so, I shall invite you to give me an introduction to two people whom you think might well benefit from a similar interview. Would you have any objections to that?"

This opening puts your prospect at ease. First of all he realises you have not got some pre-conceived idea of what you are going to sell him. Second, he knows you are going to be good because otherwise he won't give you any introductions. Third, as you are going through the factfind you may find your prospect will jot down the name of someone who occurs to him when you ask a particular question. I have had this happen quite frequently when something I have said has reminded him of a conversation he may have had with one of his friends in recent days. At the end of your meeting you refer back to your opening statement, and ask if he is now willing to give you two names as promised.

11. MY FEE

It never seems to occur to the life insurance agent that his prospect may be uncertain as to whether or not a fee will be charged for the services provided. You can turn this uncertainty to your advantage.

"Mr Prospect, I must tell you that I do charge a fee for my services, but strangely enough it will not cost you any money. All I ask in return for the conversation we are about to have, is that you introduce me to two people who you think might be interested in what I have to offer. I am sure you appreciate the only way I can develop my business is by expanding my client bank; therefore I have introduced this rather unique fee charging system which I am sure you will find acceptable."

12. THE PERSONAL TELEPHONE DIRECTORY

When you take on a new client you give him one of your business cards. The chances are in two or three weeks it will be lost.

Ask for your client's telephone directory and write your name, address and telephone number in it. As you hand the book back, say to him: "John, I am sure there are a number of people in here who have need of my services. Would you take a few moments to go through it and pick out the ones you think would most benefit from a conversation with me?" Alternatively, a number of families have birthday books where the same approach can be used.

13. PROSPECT LISTS

During your conversation with prospects, if you are truly listening you will be surprised at how many names they will give you, either directly or indirectly. For example, your prospect reveals his hobby is squash. You naturally show interest and he tells you about the current club competition and the names of the people he is playing against.

Three months later you pop back to see him, taking with you a list of names. In the list you include the people he told you about, and say, "John, would you mind looking through my list because these are the people I want to meet within the next two weeks or so. I was just wondering if there is anyone on it you know, and to whom you could give me an introduction?" Surprise, surprise, there is and all you need to do is ask his permission to use his name as one of your clients when you make contact.

14. A 20 MINUTE INTERVIEW

If you accept that everyone you meet is a potential client, the only problem is how to get them to sit down and talk to you. Try this one:

"Would you have any objection to spending 20 minutes talking with me about your life insurance programme (or of course it could be your pension, investment, or health insurance programmes)?" The likely response is, "I have no real objection to spending 20 minutes talking to you, but I don't honestly think there is anything I need." You have got your appointment and now it's down to you.

15. SHAREHOLDERS LISTS

There are a number of commercial organisations which market lists of shareholders in public companies. You need to define your 'target market' with some care to ensure you get the quality of prospects you want and in the right geographic location. These lists can be used for direct approach or seminar invitations; without doubt they are a lucrative source of quality prospects.

16. PLANNING APPLICATIONS

Very few people realise the information which is available from their own local authority.

Most authorities publish the details of current planning applications in the local press, but why wait for that? You can go into the planning department and ask to see the Planning Register. You are at liberty to extract information about people who have applied for planning permission and, therefore, will be spending money on new buildings or extensions. The list will include commercial as well as private development and if you really want to follow it through, you could actually sit in the public gallery during the committee meeting when the individual applications are being considered. When you make contact with the selected prospects they are bound to be impressed at the trouble you have taken, and the knowledge you have of their plans, which should lead to a fruitful discussion about the way in which you might be able to help them achieve their objectives.

The Business Market

What about business insurance? No doubt some of the people you meet through domestic prospecting will be self-employed or running their own businesses, and that is one way to get into the corporate market. Here are some more specific prospecting methods.

17. LOCAL ADVERTISING FOR JOB VACANCIES

Look through your local paper at the employment vacancies being offered. If there is no mention of pension provision, why not telephone the personnel manager and suggest to him the response to his advertisement might be improved if he was able to offer the benefits of a company pension scheme? Now, of course, you may find a scheme is in existence and he simply omitted to mention it in the advertisement. In that case you have a golden opportunity to talk about additional voluntary contributions.

If there is no scheme in force, however, surely you are the person to go along and tell him all about it?

18. TRADE REGISTERS

There is a plethora of trade and industrial registers on the market. The best contain comprehensive company information, including turnover, year end and directors' names. How you use the information is up to you. A cold mail shot approach may not be the best method. You really need to find someone who can give you an introduction.

19. HOW TO GET AN INTRODUCTION

Having gone through your trade register and extracted a list of companies to contact, look through your client bank and network of acquaintances. Do you know anyone who can give you an introduction to those companies?

For example, you may have a manufacturer amongst your clients who is likely to be using materials supplied by one of the companies on your list. Show the list around. Somebody, somewhere, can almost certainly give you an introduction to the directors, which is far better than a cold mailshot approach.

20. NEW COMPANY REGISTRATIONS

One hundred and twenty thousand new companies are launched every year and although some of them are subsidiaries of existing organisations there are plenty of start-up situations.

If you could only find out who these companies are, you might well be the first insurance man to talk to them. Of course you can find out, because there are organisations who will sell you a list of new company registrations in your locations.

A direct approach would be preferable to a mailshot letter. Again look for a possible introducer within your own client bank.

21. PROSPECTING THROUGH COMPANY ACCOUNTS

The annual returns of limited companies must be registered with Companies House and, as a result of pressure from the Inland Revenue, returns tend to be much more up to date than was formally the case. They contain a wealth of information about the company and the directors, and can, therefore, be a particularly useful prospecting tool.

You need to learn how to interpret accounts and a lesson from your own accountant will show you what to look for.

You still have to make the appointment, but your analysis of the company accounts may well enable you to target in on a key area. Most company directors would be impressed at the trouble you have taken to find out about the company, although on rare occasions some may take offence — probably because you demonstrated you know more about certain aspects of the company than they know themselves.

22. YELLOW PAGES

You could just get hold of the Yellow Pages classified directory, extract all the electricians and write them a cold approach letter. Do not expect a very good response.

Alternatively, show the same list to one of your clients who just happens to be an electrician himself. "John, tell me, do you know anything about the other electricians on this list?" Of course he does, and he will tell you who is doing well and who isn't. What a wonderful approach to ring up those who are doing well, and say, "You won't know me but my client, Bill Sparks, has told me you are one of the best electricians in town, I think I am one of the best insurance agents in town. May I come along and show you the sort of thing I do for my clients?" You have given him what the behavioural scientists call a 'stroke' by saying something nice about him, and it really does enhance the probability of getting an appointment.

On the other hand you could show the same list to one of your builder clients. He almost certainly will know one or two electricians and the same scenario would apply.

Then extend the system to other allied trades, utilising your existing client bank as your source of introduction. This is creative use of Yellow Pages.

23. CHAMBER OF COMMERCE

Join your local chamber of commerce. All good business houses in the area will be members. There will be an opportunity to attend the monthly business meeting and, if you are so inclined, to get involved with committee work. You will have the mailing list of all the other members which you can freely use.

My own local chamber has a market place luncheon every quarter when four members, drawn from the hat at the previous market place meeting, are given six minutes to promote themselves. The chosen have a wonderful opportunity to 'sell themselves' under the most favourable circumstances possible.

24. ARRANGE A CORPORATE SURVEY

With the permission of my local chamber I conducted a corporate survey, the objective of which was to present to potential commercial lenders the vibrant business scene in my local area. I wanted to upgrade their image of business in my town in order to encourage investment.

I had an extremely good response; the results were published in the local paper and on television, and all people who participated received a copy of the detailed analysis.

One question I included on my survey was the date of the company year end and I also asked about pension arrangements. The companies concerned were most receptive when I followed up over the next 12 months and talked about pension arrangements, keyman and corporate life insurance cover. Substantial business resulted.

25. A YEAR END INDEX

Build up a year end index as you are prospecting in the corporate market. As you well know, investment into pension policies is one of the few remaining tax saving opportunities available to limited companies, but the premium has to be paid in the year in which tax relief is to be claimed. This gives us a unique marketing opportunity which we should not overlook.

26. EMPLOYEE COUNSELLING

It is not unusual for companies to make financial advice available to their senior executives, and to 'sell' this as a perk. There is no reason at all why similar counselling should not be made available to the majority of a company's workforce; if properly marketed by the directors, it can be perceived by the employees as an attractive benefit.

A good firm will make a room available to you for, say, a day a month and will put round some publicity to their employees telling them you are on site.

27. REDUNDANCY COUNSELLING

Redundancy is undoubtedly here to stay. People who have had no previous experience in handling comparatively large sums of money, can find themselves in possession of substantial sums and need advice on what to do. Redundancy is certainly a major turning point in the lives of many people, and the experience is not unlike bereavement. The initial reaction is shock, followed quickly by sorrow and then anger. Ultimately, however, there is the need to pick up the threads of life once more.

Next time you see an announcement in your local paper about redundancies, why not telephone the personnel manager and offer your services? Make sure you become knowledgeable about State benefits because questions will be asked, and you need the information in order to help design solutions to the financial problems your potential clients will have.

I have been involved in a number of major company redundancies and it has been some of the most satisfying work I have ever undertaken.

28. SPONSORSHIP

You can spend a lot of money on sponsorship and not always get a good return, so you need to understand what is involved, and be selective in the organisations you agree to support.

Some years ago I sponsored the local point to point for three seasons. The average 'gate' was around 6,000 and included some of the wealthiest people in the county. As the major sponsor my name was well publicised and I have no doubt my investment was profitable.

You must be clear in your own mind why you are sponsoring the event or organisation. Is it that you simply want to help, or are you looking on it as a business opportunity? There is a fundamental difference in approach and it is most important that both you and the organisation understand your objective. Properly used, the results of sponsorship can be attractive and I believe we shall see more of it in the future.

29. BECOME A PUBLIC SPEAKER

Most organisations are no different from the Life Insurance Association. They have monthly meetings and are always looking for speakers. Develop a talk on your specialist subject. Contact local organisations and offer to speak for them.

I have spoken at a number of meetings for young farmers' clubs in the area, to the National Association of Widows, Rotary and Round Table. It is a wonderful way of getting known and meeting new people.

30. USE YOUR NETWORK

Whether you realise it or not you have built up a network of contacts. Perhaps they are people you were at school with or university, or fellow members of clubs or associations. Many of them are part of your personal network; not only do you know them, they know you. Use your networks.

31. HELP FROM YOUR ACCOUNTANT

Many companies use their accountant's address as their registered office. Outside his office will be a board containing a list of these companies. The next time you go in to see him, spend a few moments jotting down some of the names. Plan an approach to those companies. During your preamble or perhaps at some point in your factfind you will naturally ask the name and address of their accountant. "What a coincidence. They are my accountants as well. Who deals with your affairs?"

The fact that you use the same accountant gives you credibility. Possibly even more important, it gets over the difficulties we can sometime experience if our prospect wants to refer recommendations to his accountant. It would be perfectly natural for you to say, "May I have permission to discuss my recommendations with your accountant?"

Now for the bonus. When you talk to the accountant about your proposals there is no chance whatsoever he will discuss them with another financial adviser, thus possibly depriving you of the business you so richly deserve.

32. PRODUCE YOUR OWN BROCHURE

Create your own brochure, portraying your business and professional image to the world at large. You could arrange for a public relations firm to do it for you, but frankly it is better to write it yourself. It needs to be very professional and designed to fit in a letter-sized envelope so that you can use it in prospecting.

Remember, the brochure will be perceived to be you in printed form. Therefore, it needs to be really good to ensure people get the right impression of you and the work you do.

33. PRODUCE A NEWSLETTER

Your existing client bank is a goldmine. You need to stay in touch. One of the easiest ways is by using a newsletter containing general interest articles about the economy, tax and legislation issues, and investment ideas. You can either write it yourself, or there are proprietary versions available which can be over-printed with your name, address and personal message.

You could also put your better quality prospects on your mailing list which will enable you to keep in touch, and at the same time allow them to 'get to know you'. If you write the newsletter yourself you can include a paragraph aimed, in a subtle way, at one of your specific prospects; then follow it up with a phone call.

The newsletter must look very professional otherwise it will do you more harm than good. It is better to spend a few extra pounds to get a quality job than to economise and produce an inferior product.

34. FAMILY SEMINARS

Select one of your clients who is a 'centre of influence'. Suggest he invites 10 of his friends and their wives to an informal supper at which you will be the guest speaker. On the night you will be introduced by the host and will make a simple presentation on the key elements of long term financial planning. If you brief your host properly he will, in his vote of thanks at the end of your presentation, ask if you are willing to contact each of his guests in case they would like to have a personal meeting with you. You pay the costs of the evening, which will be quite modest, yet the returns will be excellent.

35. LUNCHTIME SEMINARS

Invite some of your professional contacts to a lunchtime seminar when you are launching a new product or wish to explain the industry's reaction to changes in tax or Government legislation. This will be another brief, low budget affair, probably well attended and very useful in cementing relations with your professional contacts as well as producing specific leads.

36. INVESTMENT SEMINARS

Put on an investment and inheritance tax seminar inviting everyone on the shareholders list you purchased. You might well find between 5 per cent and 10 per cent will accept your invitation for a meeting which will be held in the morning in one of the best local hotels. Your professionally prepared presentation could well generate substantial business.

37. GETTING TO KNOW YOU

There are a number of people who are in a position to influence business your way. You cannot expect them to do so until they know something about you. At the same time you need to know something about them, to ensure the quality of the introductions they are able to give you is of the standard you require.

Why not invite them to a 'getting to know you luncheon' in your office? You can send a taxi to pick them up and promise to deliver them back to their office in time for the afternoon business. After a light buffet lunch in your 'boardroom', spend 45 minutes getting to know each other.

38. A SEMINAR FOR ONE

How about a really exclusive seminar?

Select your prospect carefully and invite him to a Seminar For One. This will take the form of a business lunch, again in your office, and you tell him in advance it will last 60 minutes. You provide a cold meal, perhaps with a glass of wine, which takes all of 20 minutes to consume. You then have 40 minutes to make your presentation.

One page 1 of a pre-prepared flip chart you list the following:

1. Keyman Scheme.
2. Personal Retirement Plan.
3. Corporation Tax Savings.
4. See-saw Scheme.
5. Executive Benefits Package.
6. Critical Illness.
7. Disability Benefits.
8. Corporate Loans.
9. Estate Preservation.

Here is your opening speech:

"In my experience there are nine areas which concern a businessman from time to time. Would you care to look through this list and tell me which is the priority item for you today?" Having made your little speech you do what most salesmen find extremely difficult — close your mouth and say nothing!

After a few moments study, your guest will select one of the items — it may be 'See-saw Scheme'. Behind your facing sheet you have pre-prepared presentations for each of the nine items on your list. Whichever heading he selects you can instantly produce the appropriate visual aid and go straight into a sales presentation. In fact, the moment he makes his selection you are in a closing interview.

39. ARRANGE A FINANCIAL WEEKEND

I hired a complete leisure centre in a nearby seaside resort and put on a financial weekend. We had a variety of displays, a series of brief seminars and videos showing throughout the entire complex. A number of advisers were on hand to deal with enquiries and we had a draw to secure prospects' names and addresses. With just one advertisement in the local paper we attracted more than 2,500 people. Some drove as far as 60 miles to talk to us about their investments.

The cost? Not a great deal really. There was the hire charge for the centre, surprisingly less than you would expect, and food and drink for the staff in attendance. We had a draw with £500 of unit trusts as the prize and the meeting cost in total, around £1,500. You have to speculate to accumulate and we certainly did extremely well out of that particular function.

40. TRADE SHOWS

Your local chamber of commerce and other organisations put on trade shows. Organisers do all the publicity for you, and all you have to do is take a stand. You will have the public come to visit you and during quiet moments have the opportunity to wander around speaking to other stand holders. The latter will probably produce more business for you than the visiting public but does that matter?

41. TAKE A STAND AT YOUR LOCAL AGRICULTURAL SHOW

If you are fortunate enough to have an agricultural show in your area, consider taking a stand. The show will be visited by the farming fraternity within a 50 mile radius. They tend to make it a day out, bringing the whole family with them. They don't want to spend all their time looking at tractors and combine harvesters!

A day at an agricultural show can be very tiring. There is nothing visitors like better than an opportunity to sit down, put their feet up, have a nice cup of tea and a friendly chat to somebody about pensions, inheritance tax, investments and even life assurance. If you want to ensure your stand is kept particularly busy have a draw offering a really good prize. You will get a lot of names and addresses to follow up afterwards.

42. GET INVITED TO CLIENTS' FUNCTIONS

We are not the only people to put on seminars, trade stand exhibitions and the like. Our clients do as well. Engineer invitations to their functions. They are an ideal place to meet prospects and it costs you nothing to be there.

43. ANOTHER QUICKIE

"John, would you like to consider becoming one of my clients?" Nobody has ever asked him that before and the uniqueness of your approach may well win the day when something more formal would get a rejection.

44. PAY FOR ALL THE COFFEE IN YOUR FAVOURITE RESTAURANT FOR ONE DAY

In any town you will find a restaurant where the business people tend to congregate for morning coffee. Make an arrangement with the proprietor that you will pay for all the coffee drunk in his restaurant on one selected day, or if you are feeling particularly generous, the whole week! You have a poster up telling everybody you are providing the coffee, and the only thing they have to do is to give up their business card.

Alternatively, you could go to your local hotel and do the same 'deal' for lunch coffee. You will get a lot of publicity, give people pleasure, they will admire your ingenuity and innovative approach, and who knows some of them will probably agree to a business meeting.

Now For Some Sales Ideas

So there are 44 prospecting ideas, some old, some new, some you have tried, others you haven't. Confucius said, "You never step in the same river twice." An idea first heard maybe 10 years ago was not suitable to the way you were working at the time. Today, like a bolt of lighting it hits you, and you can use it. Here is a selection of some of the best sales ideas I have come across.

45. WOULD YOU COME AND WORK FOR ME?

In my experience few people have a true appreciation of the amount of life assurance cover they require. This may be our fault for not making the position clear to them. Here is a question that will focus their attention on the key issue.

"Would you be prepared to work for me for the rest of your life for whatever you are insured for?" No one yet has said yes when I have asked that question. You follow up by saying, "Then how do you expect your family to survive when you admit that you couldn't?" If that doesn't get you into a meaningful discussion, nothing will.

46. LIFE ASSURANCE ON STRANGERS

"How much life assurance do you have?" Write the figure down.

Second question. "Do you have a comprehensive policy on your house?" Usually people do, and you write down one million pounds.

"Contents insurance?" Another million. "Insurance on your car?" Yet another million.

"John, I am a little mystified. You have only X amount of insurance on your own life, and yet in excess of three million pounds on the lives of total strangers." When he expresses surprise, you explain briefly the cover for personal liability under his building, contents and motor insurance policies (some of which, of course, is unlimited) and draw the comparison with his own situation. It will open his mind to the need for more realistic cover on his own life.

47. CAPITAL NEEDS ANALYSIS

We really need to illustrate this one with a simple drawing. This is what it looks like and these are the words you use.

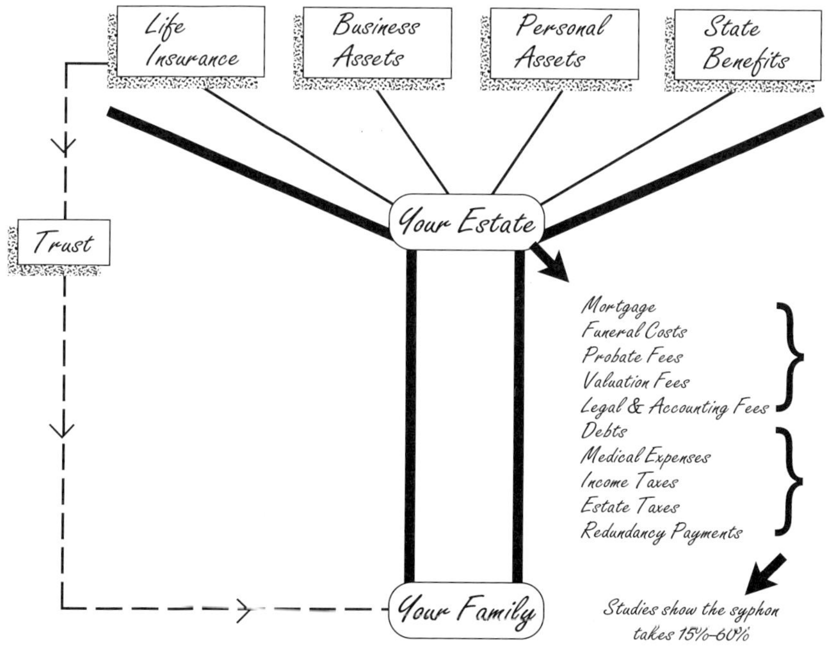

"Mr Prospect, the average man thinks that in the event of his death this is what happens:

All his life insurance, his business assets and his personal effects and any State benefits are gathered together by his solicitor; they then proceed 'down the funnel' to be collected by the family.

"This is the real situation. Just where the arrow is, cash is being syphoned off for mortgage payments, funeral costs, valuation fees, debts, medical expenses, income taxes, even redundancy payments. Our statistics show that between 15 per cent — 60 per cent of a man's estate is syphoned off in this way.

"John, there is a way around it. A very simple way. What I would like you to do is set aside a package of money that will avoid this situation completely.

"We just put the package of money into a special box called a Trust; that Trust is for your family and will be available in a matter of days should the need arise. While the hassle and arguments are going on about the mortgage and all the other matters, the family, at least, doesn't have any financial worry.

"So John, how much would you like to put in your Trust?"

48. DAYTIME APPOINTMENTS

Solicitors very rarely have evening appointments. Neither do accountants, bank managers or architects. Why do we? Because we ask for them!

Try this. Next time you are setting up an appointment, say to your prospect. "What time of day is it best for you and I to meet — morning or afternoon?" Almost everyone can find time for meetings during the day it if is important enough, and if he believes it is the only time such meetings can take place. He will find the time. All you have to do is ask, and you will get the vast majority of your appointments during the day.

49. HAVE MEETINGS IN YOUR OFFICE

Having established the most convenient time is the morning, your next question is, "Do you know where my office is?" Up until now your prospect, particularly in the domestic market, may well have thought you were going to his house. Now, as though it were a matter of form, you have shown that such meetings take place in your office. Should your prospect express surprise that you are not visiting him, you simply explain you have all the facilities in the office to help you solve whatever problems he may have.

50. AGENDAS

Prepare an agenda for almost every prospect or client meeting you have. If possible send one prior to the meeting to all those who will attend. Alternatively, see that each person has a copy when they arrive. Apart from the benefit in time management terms, you will be in charge of the meeting (having set the agenda) and have no difficulty in introducing discussion on the various items which require attention.

51. WHY DID YOU GRANT ME THIS INTERVIEW?

The last thing people expect is the unexpected! Try opening your next factfind meeting with a very unusual question. "John, before we start may I ask what made you agree to this appointment?" You may be surprised at his reply!

He might say because you were persistent! You could take that as a type of backhanded compliment! On the other hand you could suddenly find yourself straight into a closing interview. "Well, you did mention mortgages and I am just about to buy a property. I have been recommended to do my loan on the endowment basis, but I read in my newspaper recently that using a pension policy might be better. Can you tell me something about it?"

An unusual approach can often 'break the ice' and lead you into some interesting situations.

52. WOULD YOU BE WILLING TO TAKE A DROP IN SALARY?

You do not have to be in our business for very long before you start hearing objections. Interestingly enough, many an objection is really a buying signal if you only read it that way.

For example, how many times have you heard people say, "I like your idea; I know I should do something about it but I just cannot afford it." That really is not an objection because the prospect has shown quite clearly he wants to buy your solution to his problem.

In appropriate circumstances try this response:

"John, I appreciate your concern. Let me paint a picture which may help you change your mind.

"I know you have a good job at the moment, but we do frequently hear of sudden and unexpected redundancies. What if you received a letter tomorrow from your employer stating that due to a fall off in sales it is essential to economise and, as a result, a number of people would have to be made redundant, including you?"

However, there is a PS to the letter. "There is one way in which we are able to safeguard your job. If you are willing to take a cut in salary of £1,000 a year, your future would be assured. John, would you and your family be able to survive on that reduced income?"

I suspect the answer every time would be yes, although it might be difficult.

"Fortunately, as far as we know John, that letter is not in the post to you, but is it not just as important for you to sacrifice at least some of that £1,000 in order to safeguard the financial future of your wife and children?"

Finding the premium is often a question of priorities. If your prospect can truly see the logic of your proposals, he is more likely to find the premium to pay for them.

53. INDEX LINK EVERYTHING

Remember the Rule of 72. Divide 72 by the inflation rate and the answer will be the number of years it takes money to halve in purchasing power. Assuming an inflation rate of 7 per cent per annum, £10,000 today will buy only £5,000 worth of goods in 10 years' time.

A life assurance or pension policy written in today's terms only will clearly prove inadequate. You will do your client no favour at all by saving him a penny or two today at a cost of many hundreds of pounds tomorrow. So the rule is, index link everything you can.

Where life cover is involved you would also be giving him an element of guaranteed insurability for all time whatever happens to his state of health. I often wonder how industry can offer such outstanding benefits at so little cost!

54. ANNUAL PREMIUMS

Always start off by quoting annual premiums. Sometimes people pay them! You may know from your factfind that there is money in the building society and, therefore, cash is available. There are also those who do not like to have direct debits going through their account month after month.

I must say, though, most times the conversation goes something like this: "Ken, I do like your solution and I agree I need it, but to lay out £1,000 in a lump sum is going to be difficult for me. Can I pay monthly?" "Of course you can, John. Would you feel comfortable with £100 per month?" With this simple process your client, if he accepts your proposal, can enjoy an increase of 20 per cent in his life assurance cover or pension policy, and that has to be good news for him.

55. THE MILLION POUND POLICY

Very few people have ever sold a million pound policy. Why not? Because they have not asked anybody to buy one! There are many people around who have a need for one million pounds of life assurance cover, and for which they (or someone else) might be prepared to pay the premium. The question is how do you find them?

Over the next few weeks make a list of people who you think might well come into that category. It does not matter if you do not know them personally. Carry the list around with you at all times and show it to people. "Do you know anyone on this list, and if so, is it possible you would be able to introduce me to them?" The most unlikely people can sometimes arrange an introduction.

I helped one of my clients start up a small private car hire business and one day he was taken me to the airport. I told him of my list and showed it to him. To my surprise he pointed to one name and said, "Yesterday that man was sitting where you are today. As a matter of fact he is coming with me to the gun club in two weeks' time." Who would have thought it? Where do you think I was two weeks later?

56. SALARY SACRIFICE

This is an alternative answer to the 'I can't afford it' response. "John, let us assume you are thinking of changing your job, and you have seen two advertisements in the paper which appear to be identical. One is offering a salary of £15,000 a year, a company car, subsidised mortgage and private health insurance. The salary for the second job is £14,500 a year.

"However, in addition to the same fringe benefits this employer is also guaranteeing your income to age 65 even if you are unable to work through illness or accident. Which offer would you find most attractive?"

Any prudent man would have to say the second one; and really that is all you might be asking him to do, take a drop in income of £500 a year to pay for disability insurance.

57. MORTGAGE RELATED BUSINESS

Knock on every door where you see a 'for sale' sign and offer your services.

58. PROTECT EVERY MORTGAGE YOU PLACE WITH DISABILITY INSURANCE

When arranging mortgages in future and quoting life assurance cover, automatically include the premium for full disability insurance. Do not sell the disability insurance as an 'add on'. Your client is much more likely to buy the cover if you quote him an all-in premium.

59. MORTGAGES AND CRITICAL ILLNESS COVER

Borrowing money inevitably brings with it some degree of pressure, and pressure creates tension and stress. If the borrower is unfortunate enough to suffer a critical illness he will almost certainly need to change his lifestyle. Getting rid of the stress of borrowed money would certainly help.

In addition to the inclusion of disability insurance in your mortgage cover quotations, there is a strong argument in favour of

including critical illness insurance. Remember, it is our resp
to advise clients what they should do. It is their responsi
decide whether or not they want to do it.

60. THE CORPORATE CHEQUE BOOK

Why do people want to get into the corporate market? Certainly it gets you away from evening calls, because most appointments take place in the day; also the season is 12 months, whereas the domestic market ebbs and flows due to the expensive interruptions of Christmas and family holidays.

Third, and probably the most significant reason, corporate cheque books are larger than personal ones. Why? Because the cheques are for larger amounts. What you have in your personal bank account is 'real money'. Spending it seems far more painful than writing cheques on the business account.

61. OVERDRAFT INSURANCE

Script of a conversation with a corporate business owner:

"May I ask you a few simple questions? Does your firm carry fire insurance? Public liability insurance? Employer's liability cover? Motor insurance on your vehicles?" Four questions, four affirmative answers, and by now you can probably detect some exasperation and irritation in his replies. "Overdraft insurance?" "I beg your pardon?" Now you have him really intrigued because clearly he has never heard of it.

"Mr Businessman, I am assuming that you have an overdraft from time to time and, in my experience, it is rare for companies to have overdraft insurance. In fact, it is probably the most important insurance of all, and I would like to explain to you why this is the case. Could I call to see you next Thursday at 10 am or would Friday be more convenient?"

The most valuable resource in a business is the people who run it. Loans and overdrafts are made available by lenders mainly on the basis of the confidence they have in the people running the enterprise. Take the people away and the lender will become apprehensive about the future of the business and the security of his investment. We can underwrite the loan with suitable life assurance cover.

62. HOW MANY TIMES HAVE YOU SIGNED FOR YOUR BANK OVERDRAFT?

This is the question you ask a corporate man when Idea 61 has procured an appointment.

Chances are he will not understand the question. "Would I not be right in assuming you have signed one guarantee as a director of the company and, secondly, provided a personal joint and several guarantee? If so, what you have effectively done is to place the lender ahead of your family.

"In the event of your untimely death, the lender would be satisfied first. Only if there is anything left over will your family benefit. Is that what you want?"

Of course it isn't. You then show him how you can take that problem away, and put his family first, by arranging a corporate life assurance policy, covering the company's maximum borrowing at any one time.

63. A SELF CANCELLING LOAN

Alternatively, you could say to the corporate business owner, "I understand you have a loan. Is it the self cancelling variety?"

You go on to explain that by paying an extra one, or perhaps one and a half per cent for the loan you can ensure that in the event of his death, it would automatically be cancelled. Should he hesitate over the cost, ask him what he would do if the bank was to increase his interest rate by 1.5 per cent. Would that force him out of business or could he somehow cover the increased payments?

64. WHY DID YOU GO INTO BUSINESS?

One reason people start their own business is because they want freedom and independence to 'do their own thing', but almost certainly the main reason is to make more money.

"Presumably it was not to pay the maximum amount of tax, nor merely to provide jobs for other people. Are you sure you have your priorities right? Are you putting yourself at the front of the queue or at the back? Why don't we examine your situation to see if you have your priorities right?"

65. YOUR IDEAL TERMS OF SERVICE

"Mr Prospect, if for any reason you decide to close down your business and become an employee, what terms of service would you set as your minimum requirement?"

A large salary, of course, a pension scheme providing two thirds of final salary, four times life assurance cover, maximum widow's death in service and death in retirement benefit, full disability insurance and private health care cover. "If those are so important to you Mr Prospect, why do you not provide them for yourself now, in your own business?"

66. THREE BENEFICIARIES

"Mr Prospect, there are three beneficiaries of the results of your enterprise. One is the company, the second is you, and the third is the Inland Revenue. If I could take just one of those three away from you, which one would it be?"

Unless you are dealing with a very strange man he will say the Revenue, which would give you the opportunity to talk about the tax efficiency of directors pension arrangements.

67. WHAT ARE YOU WORTH TO THE COMPANY?

Probably a great deal more than he has ever realised. He is almost certainly the number one keyman. Company premises are replaceable; he is not. Company premises are insured for their full replacement value, he does not even know what his is. Perhaps you can help him find out.

68. OWNERSHIP OF THE BUSINESS

"Let me ask you three simple questions.
Who owns the business?
Who should own the business?
Who will own the business?"

How many participants in a business enterprise know what would happen to the shares of a deceased director? You and I know that, in the absence of any agreement, they would almost certainly pass to the director's widow. She would not want them, preferring to have cash. It is unlikely the surviving directors would be particularly happy to have the deceased director's widow as a principal shareholder in the company. Cash would solve the problem, but in the absence of any specific provision it might be difficult, if not impossible, for the surviving directors to acquire the shareholding. Life insurance puts money in the right hands at the right time.

69. I WANT TO BUY YOUR BUSINESS

Technically, there are a number of ways in which a business can be valued. At the end of the day the accountant is probably the only person who can give you the correct figure. But if you want to open up a discussion on share purchase, one way is to pull out your cheque book and offer to buy the business.

It is quite amazing to watch the reaction of the directors or partners. At first they do not believe their luck! Then they wonder if it is a serious offer and begin to debate amongst themselves what price they would require. Once they come back to you with a figure, the sale is made. "John, Graham, what you are telling me is you consider your business is worth £500,000. As you hold 50 per cent of the business each, your individual shareholding is worth a quarter of a million pounds. John, if Graham had died last night would you have a quarter of a million pounds immediately available to buy his shares from his widow?" It would be surprising if he were able to answer yes, and so you are able to move on to Idea 70.

70. HOW WOULD YOU RAISE THE MONEY?

Borrow it from the bank might be the first answer, to which you would point out it would cost perhaps bank rate plus 2 per cent.

The second alternative they might suggest would be to raise a mortgage on their home. Not as expensive as the bank borrowing method, but still costing anything between 12 per cent and 15 per cent.

The third alternative could be to sell an asset. If you write the asset down over 10 years and allow for the loss of earnings, the probable cost is 15 per cent.

"If I could show you a way of raising the money at a cost of 1 to 1.5 per cent per annum, would you be interested?" If the answer is no, walk out — you are not in the presence of astute businessmen.

71. THE COMPANY WILL

Another conversation stopping question. "Do you have a company Will?" Your prospect will look puzzled until you explain you are talking about what would happen to the shares of a deceased director or a major shareholder. It is another way of getting into a discussion on share protection insurance.

72. THE TWO DIARY CONCEPT

Try asking your corporate prospect to review with you the last 14 working days in his diary. Almost certainly you will find many instances where he was at his desk early in the morning and did not return home until perhaps 7 pm or later in the evening. What was the key factor that made this lifestyle for him? Almost certainly a wife who took responsibility for the personal side of his life.

Invite him to picture what his diary would be like if his wife was to die. Who would do the school run in the morning? How about collecting the children at the end of the day and looking after them at home? Could he find time to take them to the doctor when they were ill or the dentist when they needed treatment or shopping to replace their outgrown clothes?

David was a motor mechanic who serviced my car. His young wife died six weeks after the birth of their third child and, for the next five years, David hardly saw his children from Monday to Friday. When he finally remarried it was a matter of priority to arrange life insurance cover on his new wife.

73. HOW WOULD YOU FEEL ABOUT BECOMING A HOUSE-HUSBAND?

We admire the woman who makes a successful career in business. At the present time we raise an eyebrow at the man who becomes a house-husband even though it may not be his fault.

Just try asking a businessman, "How do you feel about becoming a house-husband?" He will not be very excited at the prospect and you have the means within your briefcase to ensure it does not happen.

74. WHO ARE THE KEY PEOPLE IN YOUR ORGANISATION?

Ask this question and you will hear about the financial director, the sales director, the designer, the accountant and whoever else the boss thinks makes a contribution to the company's profits.

One person he will almost certainly overlook, perhaps through modesty, is himself. If he is not crucial to the business what on earth is he doing sitting in the chief executive's chair?

He is also not likely to include his wife, so your simple question can produce not one, but two potential prospects.

75. WHAT ARE YOU DOING TO STOP YOUR KEYMAN LEAVING?

He will tell you, underlining the value of the man to the organisation, and the benefits he is providing to persuade him to stay.

Does the keyman himself realise the value the company places on him? If not he might well be attracted by a competitor's offer and move on. This would clearly hurt the company and it would be in their interests to ensure his benefit package was the best the company could afford — and that he knows what it is worth.

76. WHY DON'T YOU PAY YOUR KEYMAN LESS?

When you ask this question, do not be surprised if your client looks at you as though you are mad. "Because he would leave me, of course."

"Would that cause you some problems?" "Of course it would, he is extremely valuable to the company and makes a significant contribution to our profitability." "In that case, would it not be sensible for the company to arrange substantial life assurance on him, because if he left you not of his own free will, but because of an untimely death, the company's loss would be just as great. I suggest the company considers effecting a life assurance policy for say, two years' salary, which would provide a cash cushion allowing the business to recover the loss it would clearly experience."

77. THE KEYMAN AND HIS CAR

During a factfind with a corporate owner he tells you one of the keymen is his sales director and amongst his benefits, quite naturally, is a company car.

"If your sales director was involved in an accident and both he and the company car were a total loss, which would be the most difficult to replace?" Obviously, the keyman. "Of the two, which have you got insured for the full replacement value?" Again almost equally obviously, the company car. The moment you ask the question your prospect will realise the stupidity of the answer, and you are into a closing interview.

78. RE-FINANCING LOANS

How many young solicitors, accountants and architects do you know who prove impervious to your persuasiveness and fail to take out a personal retirement plan? The usual reason they give is the cost of educating their children at private schools.

The way many professional firms operate the partners are likely to have a substantial amount of money tied up in the capital account. If they also have enough equity in their house, you have the key to solve both their problem and yours. You unlock capital, replacing it with funds produced by an increased mortgage on their house, running alongside a pension policy, and you use the money released to finance the children's education.

79. GOODWILL AND CRITICAL ILLNESS

Those same professionals who require your help on school fees may have a goodwill element tied up in their practice. Most partnership agreements make provision for the repayment of the goodwill on retirement and, possibly, early death. The onset of a critical illness can cause major problems which we now have the ability to solve.

80. COMMERCIAL LOANS AND CRITICAL ILLNESS

It is common practice for commercial and partnership loans to be covered by life assurance. The cost of critical illness cover on the total loan may be prohibitive and a compromise is to suggest each partner or director is covered under a critical illness policy for two years' interest on the loan. This would 'buy time', allowing the business an opportunity to recover from the immediate effects which it would feel following the loss of one of the key contributors to the enterprise.

81. QUOTE PERCENTAGES

You and I both know the incredible impact of compound interest and what this can do to the projected benefits in our pension plan illustrations. Unfortunately, the public do not, and the massive 'projected funds' carry little or no credibility. They simply look like telephone numbers.

For this reason it is far better to illustrate projected benefits under a pension policy as a percentage of projected final salary. This puts some real meaning into your illustrations and will help your client make the right buying decision. It places the whole matter into the correct perspective when he can see, for example, that his final pension is likely to be only 10 per cent or 15 per cent of final salary.

82. TALK PAY DAYS, NOT YEARS, TO RETIREMENT

Your prospect is 50 next birthday, and he tells you he wants to retire in 10 years' time. "Just 120 pay days away" you reply, and believe me that puts a different complexion on the whole situation.

Go on and ask him how many years he expects to live after retirement. Fifteen or 20 is a common reply – 180 or 240 pay days. The prospect begins to see the picture; he has just 120 pay days out of which he has to build up a sufficient fund to provide the income he will want in retirement for perhaps twice as long.

83. THE PENSION PYRAMID

"Mr Prospect, at retirement men will fall into one of five categories. Just a few will be incredibly rich. Rather more will be wealthy, and a substantial number will be comfortable in financial terms. Sadly a great portion will find life a major struggle and the majority will be downright poor. Which category do you intend to be in?"

One or two will say incredibly wealthy, of course, and that's good because they have immediately become a prospect for inheritance tax planning. The majority will say they plan to be comfortable; you respond with two words, "define comfortable." As they do so you will have the opportunity to check with them they are on target with their current pension planning. If not you can begin to talk about the shortfall.

A creative way to demonstrate this particular idea is to draw a pyramid.

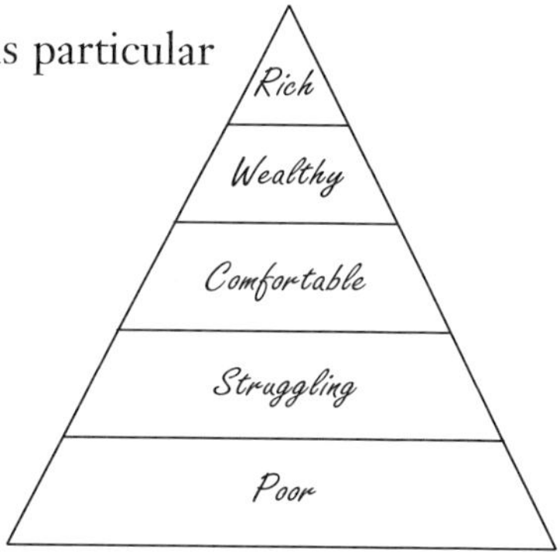

84. THE PENSION BICYCLE

The response you often get when you talk to prospects about adequate pension provision is they cannot afford it at the moment, but intend to do something about it in the future. My response is to select three local hills and draw a simple picture to demonstrate the value of starting early.

"I want you to picture yourself cycling up a hill. It's quite a gentle hill — perhaps 1 in 6. You could get up there alright on your bicycle, couldn't you? That would be the situation if you started your pension plan now.

"Should you leave it 10 years, look what happens. To get to the same point the hill is very much steeper and you have to work and pedal much harder.

ıat if you leave it, as so many people do, until age 55? It's almost .l isn't it?"

ıe later you start the harder you have to climb, and the harder you nave to pedal. That is exactly what happens if you continually put off your pension planning.

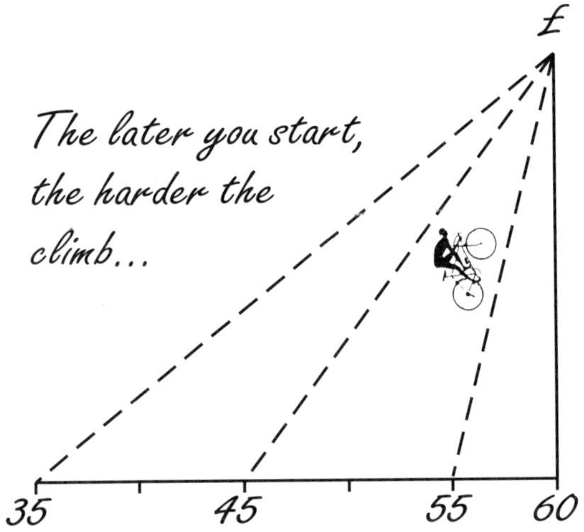

85. THE QE2

Despite your bicycle illustration, the self-employed man may well come back to you and say, "That's all very well but my business is going to be my pension."

Try this on. "Let us assume you decide to take your wife on a cruise round the Antarctic on the QE2. As you wait on the quayside to board the ship, you can't help noticing there is something different about it. When you mention it to the First Officer he explains the cruise has been over-booked because it is so popular. In order not to disappoint anybody, the company has decided to do away with lifeboats because the QE2 is such a safe ship it does not consider there is any chance of them being needed. Would you still feel happy to go on that cruise?"

Of course you wouldn't. No matter how safe the ship, the lifeboats are carried 'just in case'. However confident your client may be that he will be able to sell his business and fund his retirement, does it not make sense to have a lifeboat in the form of a pension policy, 'just in case'? I am sure you can give him examples of businessmen in your area who relied on similar planning only to find a change in the market, the opening of a new road or a major competitor in the neighbourhood reduced the value of their business overnight.

86. A DROP IN INCOME

Our prospect reaches age 60 and retirement and what happens? His income level suffers a substantial drop.

Say to your prospect, "Could you afford to give up a pound a day? Would you miss a pound a day as much as you would miss that enormous drop in income at retirement? Let me show you the effect of just giving up one pound a day now."

This simple little illustration is within anyone's capability however inadequate you may feel yourself as an artist!

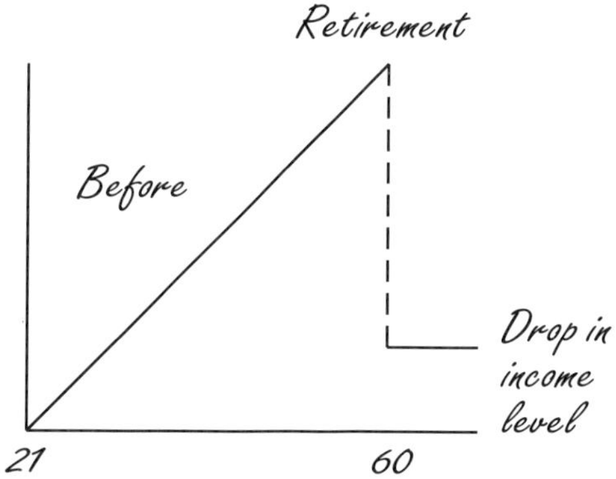

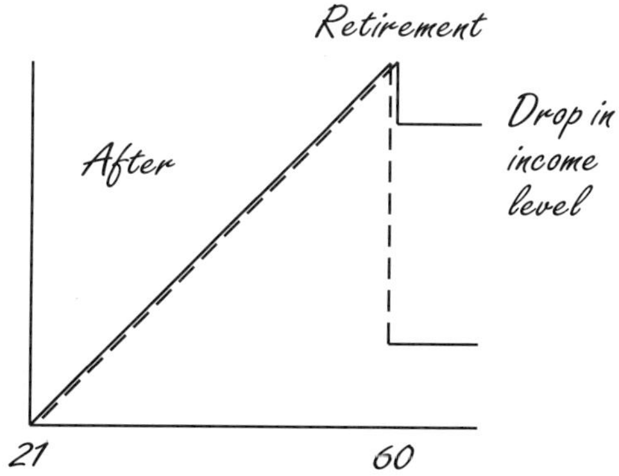

87. A PENSIONS QUICKIE

"Mr Prospect, pensions come in two sizes, big ones and little ones. Which sort do you want?"

He is bound to say big, isn't he? All you then do is ask him to define what he means by 'big'. Almost certainly it is much larger than his existing pension arrangements are going to produce.

88. A SUBSIDIARY COMPANY

Would your prospect like to set up a subsidiary company, a unique one which suffers no taxes whatsoever, requires little or no day to day management by him, but merely an annual board meeting? Even more important would he not like to feel he is actually in business with one of the country's largest financial institutions?

This is the 'subsidiary company' concept of corporate pension planning.

Company A, his main company, invests a small slice of its turnover in subsidiary company B. The subsidiary company consists of a tax free fund, which can be exchanged for an income at retirement age. It can include some inheritance tax benefits and life assurance and widow's cover can also be built in.

A simple concept and probably the most effective retirement pension plan sales illustration ever designed.

89. WHAT ABOUT WIVES?

Many wives play an active part in their husband's business. The doctor's wife acts as his receptionist. The businessman's wife is his part time secretary and social host. Their 'employer' may or may not pay them a salary.

He certainly should, of course, because it is tax efficient particularly under independent taxation. In addition he can provide them with a pension which will help his corporate and personal tax situation, and enable his wife to enjoy the benefits of tax allowance when she starts drawing on her pension fund.

There are still tremendous opportunities for this extremely simple sale.

90. THE ANNUAL BENEFITS STATEMENT

Most employers 'undersell' the fringe benefits they provide for their employees. Indeed, the employer himself may not be aware of the true cost of these benefits which are very much part of the remuneration package he is offering.

Why not offer to prepare a benefit statement in consultation with the employer, in which you list the individual items and try to 'cost' them. This may well prevent a good employee from becoming dissatisfied in comparing his own job with offers of another. Indeed, he may look at the job which appears to be worth more money when, in fact, his present pay and benefits package is far superior.

There are, of course, some statutory obligations on an employer to provide information but a company which goes no further than the law demands is being less than fair to both itself and to its employees.

From your point of view the use of this benefit statement could well help you to highlight deficiencies in the life assurance, pensions and investment programme — providing additional sales opportunities.

91. ASK YOUR PROSPECT WHAT HE WOULD DO IF HE WON A MILLION ON THE POOLS.

"Retire at once" is likely to be his reply.

"Let us say you won not a million pounds but £100,000, what then? Could you afford to retire?" After a few moments thought (converting capital into income) the answer is almost certainly no.

"On the basis of your present planning all you will have to show when you retire is a fund of £100,000. Clearly, you now think this is not adequate, and perhaps we should begin to increase it."

92. ADDITIONAL VOLUNTARY CONTRIBUTIONS

Simple 'opener' based on four straightforward questions.

Question 1: "Are you in the company pension scheme?"

Question 2: "Is your membership of the scheme important, and do you consider the potential benefits valuable?"

Question 3: "How much do you expect to receive from it when you retire?"

Question 4: "It has been my experience that there is often a difference between what people expect to receive under their pension plan, and what the benefits will actually be. Would you like me to check your understanding for you and, if there is a shortfall, would you be willing to consider discussing ways in which it could be made good?"

93. FARMERS AND THEIR INHERITANCE TAX PROBLEM

Sitting in the farm office of one of my clients, my eye was attracted by the map on the wall showing the individual farms that made up the 2,500 acres of the estate.

A question came into my mind. "John, do you mind telling me which of those farms you do not own?" My client looked puzzled, and pointed out I knew very well they had no rented land at all.

I begged to differ, and selecting one of the farms which seemed to be be about the right size said, "That's the one, John." Before he could reply I went on to explain the way in which inheritance tax works and that, effectively, around 20 per cent of the estate was 'on loan' from the capital taxes office. When inheritance tax came to be paid, it would want a sum equal to the value of the farm I had selected.

It was a truly effective way to put over a painful message and has proved its worth on more than one occasion since.

94. PAY CAPITAL TAXES OUT OF CAPITAL

Inheritance tax is a charge on capital, not income.

I explained to one of my clients his inheritance tax bill was around one million pounds. We discussed insurance cover (this was before the surviving spouse exemption) and although he was comparatively young, he felt his income was insufficient to meet the premium on the life policy.

I asked whether he was able to sign a cheque for an annual premium, taking the money out of his business assets rather than from the monthly income. The point was made, the cheque was signed and the plan put into effect. He still pays the annual premium out of his capital account rather than his personal one.

95. SEND YOUR PROSPECTS VIDEOS OR AUDIO CASSETTES

Have you thought about delivering an appropriate video or cassette to a prospect or client in advance of your meeting?

For example, at the Toronto Million Dollar Round Table meeting there was a superb presentation on disability insurance. The speaker was a dentist who had become permanently disabled as a result of a swimming accident. It was an extremely powerful and moving talk, entirely suitable to show to members of the public.

There are plenty of appropriate examples from both MDRT and the Life Insurance Association, and it is a novel approach which is extremely effective.

96. REMEMBER YOUR CLIENTS WHEN YOU ARE AT SALES CONFERENCES

In a one day sales conference you will hear at least 20 ideas. One or two will be new to you.

As you listen to the various presentations, keep your clients in mind. Remember Ben Feldman at the MDRT meeting in Hawaii. Match ideas to clients, but don't wait until you get back home even if your conference is overseas. Send a card to your client, telling him you have heard something interesting which you believe would be most appropriate to his business, and you will make contact immediately you return. He will love it, and the appointment is automatic.

97. JOIN A STUDY GROUP

The life of a salesperson can be lonely. At times you feel quite isolated and consider your difficulties unique. You run out of ideas. You have a prospect with a very difficult situation and you cannot see the way through it.

Joining a study group of your peers could well be the solution. Some of the best days of my business year are those I spend with my study group, which includes amongst its members some of the best known people in the UK life insurance industry. Our agenda is varied and open-ended. We may discuss an individual situation. Perhaps one of the members will present a case study for us to examine in-depth.

Alternatively we hear about a particularly interesting problem and see the creative solutions put forward to solve it.

There is always a buzz session built in, guaranteed to be lively with sales ideas flowing backwards and forwards. Sometimes we have a guest speaker. It is also a fun day, when for a few hours we can isolate ourselves from the daily problems and spend time with people who speak the same language.

The best study groups are those which comprise people who are givers rather than takers. You must have complete confidence and trust in each other so that full, frank and free discussion can take place.

Don't delay — get involved today.

98. JUST ONE EXTRA CALL A DAY

Work it out yourself. The average salesperson works 46 weeks, 230 days. If you can make just one extra call a day, your closing rate is 1 in 4, and your average case worth £250, you have increased your gross turnover by £14,375. If your closing rate is 1 in 3, the increase is a staggering £19,166.

99. DO YOU HATE MONDAYS?

By tradition Monday is not the best day of the week, but it is unfortunately the day the business week starts.

Why should it? Why not start your week on a Friday and always set out to make a sale on that day? You can come in on Monday morning, now the second day of the week, with a case already written, and you feel a winner. The euphoria may just get you through the worst that Monday can throw at you!

100. WHY THE FIRST OF JANUARY?

Taking idea 99 a stage further, why start your year on 1st January or, more important, why finish your year on 31st December? It's such a busy month anyway and there are so many other nice things to do. People aren't so keen to see you either.

If you geared your year to 30th November, you would have the last month to 'sweep up' and get yourself ready for the New Year.

101. A REAL YEAR HAS 13 MONTHS

As the last of my 101 best ideas I will now find you a whole extra month.

We always think there are four weeks in a month, but apart from February (other than a Leap year) that is not correct. There are four weeks and a few days.

We divide our target into 12 months because the calendar says that is how many months there are in a year. Why not make your month four weeks; you would thus get 13, not 12, months in the year.

A silly idea? Well you may say so, but it's certainly simple and, after all, it is always the simple ideas that work best!

To Summarise

So there you have it. One hundred and one tried and tested ideas to help you develop your practice and your prospects and clients to recognise some of the hazards of life against which we in the life insurance industry can provide protection.

However, each sales idea is only part of the sales process. The overriding need for a full and complete factfind remains to ensure you give best advice based upon the fullest possible knowledge of your prospect's circumstances.

CHAPTER 14

Quotable Quotes

S*OME PEOPLE SEEM* to have an uncanny ability to come up with a remark which goes right to the heart of a problem. The remarks appear to be impromptu, but in all probability the speaker has used them time and time again, gradually refining and improving them until they feel absolutely right.

It is said no author worth his salt should be without a book of quotations in his reference library because their proper use will add colour to his writing. Similarly, a collection of power phrases can become the salesperson's reference book; their judicious use will add power and punch to his presentation.

As it happens they are just as likely to have a major impact on the salesperson as they are on the listener. Here are some of my favourites:

- Having life assurance and not needing it, is better than needing it and not having it.

- Even if you are on the right track you will be run over if you just sit there.

- Success is doing the things failures don't like to do.

- Don't fear criticism if you are right — don't ignore it if you are wrong.

- Winning isn't everything, losing isn't anything.

- Big problems need big solutions.

- One day you are jerking the grapes — the next day you are sipping the wine.

- Self pity is self destruction.
- A definition of life insurance — "Cash paid to somebody some day."
- I have never met a widow who claimed her husband had too much life insurance.
- The right story will move anybody to buy insurance.
- Have I convinced you to buy or do you want some more information?
- Don't tell people your problems — 80 per cent don't care and the other 20 per cent are glad you have a problem!
- A professional is a person who does not get anywhere by accident.
- Do you want success or can you live with failure?
- The opposite of termination is determination.
- A quitter will say, "I could have done it, if."
- Success is a journey not a destination.
- Don't create problems — resolve challenges.
- Champions always come back — losers give up.
- What the mind of man can conceive and believe, man can achieve.
- No one has a prospecting problem, it's an approach problem.
- If you do not have a target you are like a ship without a rudder.
- Success is getting what you want; happiness is wanting what you get.
- How can we recognise success if we have never experienced failure?

- If you don't call on the big ones, you don't get them.
- You can't help someone get to the top without getting there yourself.
- Givers are the getters in the world.
- When there is no vision the people die.
- For those who believe, no explanation is necessary. For those who do not believe, no explanation will suffice.
- We help our clients to fulfil their dreams.
- If your thinking is sinking, so is your production.
- The door of success is always ajar.
- Today is the tomorrow you worried about yesterday.
- Standing still is the same as going backwards; when you do, someone is bound to overtake you.
- Is there any reason why we can't do business together?
- A debt should last no longer than the man who created it.
- The grass on the other side of the fence really is just as difficult to mow.
- How many no's have you heard today?
- None of us is original — we are all unique.
- Compete as often as you can.
- Nothing worthwhile comes easily.
- Risk taking is the price of opportunity.
- Make commitments rather than compromises.

- You don't write large cases, you develop them.
- Inflation diminishes purchasing power, death destroys it.
- It is not the high cost of living so much as the cost of high living.
- When the competition gets tough the first choice of the weak is to quit.
- Life assurance shifts the risks from people who don't want them to people who do.
- Buy me for an hour every year.
- If you hoot with the owls at night, don't expect to soar with the eagles during the day.
- If you don't think it's a good day, just try missing one.
- Winners win in advance.
- Motivation is an inside job.
- The people who survive are those with magnificent obsessions.
- If you don't know where you are going, you'll end up some place else. If you don't stand for something, you'll fall for anything.
- If you want to make a good life, put more into it.
- Today really is the first day of the rest of your life.

EPILOGUE

Don't Quit

MY DAD WOULD HAVE LOVED this poem. His best advice to me was, "Son, develop stickability." Throughout the years I have spent in the industry that one word has been more help to me than any other.

When things go wrong, as they sometimes will,
When the road you are trudging seems all up hill,
When the funds are low and the debts are high,
And you want to smile, but you have to sigh,
When care is pressing you down a bit,
Rest, if you must — but don't you quit.

Life is queer with its twists and turns,
As everyone of us sometimes learns,
And many a failure turns about
When he might have won if he stuck it out;
Don't give up, though the pace seems slow —
You might succeed with another blow.

Often the goal is nearer than
It seems to a faint and faltering man,
Often the struggler has given up
When he might have captured the victor's cup.
And he learned too late, when the
Night slipped down,
How close he was to the golden crown.

Success is failure turned inside out —
The silver tint of the clouds of doubt —
And you never can tell how close you are,
It may be near when it seems afar;
So stick to the fight when you're hardest hit —
It's when things seem worst that you mustn't quit.